TRAIN
TEASERS

Also by Andrew Martin

NON-FICTION FOR PROFILE BOOKS

Underground, Overground: A Passenger's History of the Tube
Belles & Whistles: Journeys Through Time on Britain's Railways
Steam Trains Today: Journeys Along Britain's Heritage Railways
Night Trains: The Rise and Fall of the Sleeper

FICTION

In the Jim Stringer railway series ...
The Necropolis Railway
The Blackpool Highflyer
The Lost Luggage Porter
Murder at Deviation Junction
Death on a Branch Line
The Last Train to Scarborough
The Somme Stations
The Baghdad Railway Club
Night Train to Jamalpur
Powder Smoke

TRAIN TEASERS

A QUIZ BOOK FOR THE
CULTURED TRAINSPOTTER

ANDREW MARTIN

P

PROFILE BOOKS

First published in Great Britain in 2022 by
Profile Books Ltd
29 Cloth Fair
London
EC1A 7JQ
www.profilebooks.com/

Designed by Jade Design

1 3 5 7 9 10 8 6 4 2

Printed and bound in Great Britain by
Clays Ltd, Elcograf S.p.A.

A CIP catalogue record for this book is available from the British Library.

ISBN 978 1 78816 394 1
eISBN 978 1 78283 638 4

CONTENTS

ROLLING STOCK

BEING A PASSENGER

COLOUR SECTION · 115

ANSWERS · 120

INTRODUCTION (AND A FEW TIPS)

The title of what follows, *Train Teasers*, is meant to reflect the fact that the book aspires to a playful, rather than an adversarial, relationship with the reader. The aim is not to catch the reader out but to encourage him or her to find the right answer.

Many of the answers are guessable by means of multiple choice or other forms of limitation. We confine ourselves to *British* railways, for example, although the 'Britishness' of a couple of questions is admittedly tenuous. Also, the questions are arranged roughly chronologically so that, even if no date is mentioned in a question, the answer is unlikely to involve some Victorian railway phenomenon if the immediately preceding question referred to the Second World War.

The book is informed by the idea that it might be more satisfying to guess the location of a statue of an eminent railway personage, based on the wording of the question, than to actually know it. And the questions are oriented towards the social, picturesque, artistic and eccentric side of Britain's railways, and away from the technical aspects, such as signalling or the various methods of electric traction (to name but two of the author's particular blind spots). So the right answers might well be lurking in the dusty corners of the averagely alert reader's mind. Of course, some railway knowledge is required, but knowledge of nineteenth- and twentieth-century social and literary history will also get the reader a long way. This is not a quiz for those who prize railway arcana for its own sake; it's for anyone who would like to engage in a conversation about railway history, mindful of the fact that in Britain it has impinged on so much other history.

It is also hoped that anyone who gets an answer wrong will be compensated by enjoyment of either the question or the answer, many of which are embellished with asides or digressions by way of a bonus. The reader's enjoyment might also be increased by a look at the Framework of Railway History provided below.

Framework of Railway History

Britain's railways developed on the principle of laissez-faire – that is, chaotically. There were many companies in the early days, and in the 'Railway Grouping' of 1923 over a hundred of these were reduced to the 'Big Four' (of which more in a minute). Readers will not usually be asked to name a pre-Grouping railway company without some assisting clues, but the names of some of them do come up: the North Eastern Railway, for example, or the Great Eastern and the Great Northern.

The names of the Big Four come up more often. They were

> The Great Western
> The London & North Eastern
> The London, Midland & Scottish
> The Southern

'Great Western' was the name of a pre-Grouping company as well as one of the Big Four. It is also the name of a modern train operating company. Another modern train operator at the time of writing (and these companies come and go at a great rate) is the London North Eastern Railway, which has almost the same name as the old London & North Eastern Railway, but without the conjunction. Both are referred to as LNER, but in this book the context will make clear which is being discussed.

In 1947, the railways were nationalised as British Railways (later called British Rail). The railways were then privatised in 1994.

As mentioned, there is not much technical detail in the book, but the reader should be aware that steam locomotives (which survived until 1968) have a serial number, and that their wheel formations are usually mentioned in the same breath. A wheel formation involves three numbers. It might be, say, 2-6-0, which means two leading wheels, six driving wheels, and no trailing wheels. Some wheel formations have a name, and a 2-6-0 is a Mogul.

Steam locomotives also usually belonged to a *Class* of engines, meaning a series of similar types built at the same time by the same company or engineer. Sometimes locomotives also have individual names, for instance *Mallard*, which was a member of the A4 Class.

Some *trains* had names, and these were known as 'named' or 'famous' trains. In recent years, with the decline of the locomotive and the rise of the multiple unit (with power units distributed along the length of a train), the distinction between a train and an engine has become blurred, but there are not many questions touching on this complication.

Readers should also keep in mind that the answer to a question about a particular line might refer to a *preserved* (or heritage) *railway*, or a line of the London Underground.

The questions are grouped into five main sections; all the answers are at the back.

PEOPLE (AND ANIMALS)

ENTREPRENEURS AND ENGINEERS

1. The carved head of which British steam pioneer is on the roof of Gare du Nord Station, Paris?

2. Was George Stephenson the father of Robert, or was Robert the father of George?

3. In 1830, George Stephenson was cross-examined by a parliamentary select committee (a frequent event in his life) about his plans for the Liverpool–Manchester Railway. Towards the end of the interview, he was asked, 'Now tell me, Mr Stephenson, will you go at thirty miles [an hour]?' Stephenson replied, 'Certainly!' What was the response of the committee?

4. George Stephenson's first locomotive was called *My Lord*. The name of his second was a north-eastern slang word for a heavy, blunt object. What was it?

5. Who, on 5 July 1841, took his first step in the leisure travel business by chartering a train to take 500 temperance supporters from Leicester to Loughborough?

6. Robert Stephenson was perpetually besieged by railway entrepreneurs wanting to sign him up to their projects. He took refuge from them behind what he metaphorically called 'the house that has no knocker'. What was this in reality?

    a. The Athenaeum Club, of which he was a member, and where discussion of business was frowned on.
    b. His yacht, *Titania*.

7. George Hudson, the Railway King, was a railway entrepreneur who in 1844 was in charge of over 1,000 miles of railway. But he was dethroned after he was discovered to be a confidence trickster: he had paid dividends out of capital, not profits. He supposedly wanted to 'Mek all t' railways come to' – which city?

8. Roughly how many cigars did Isambard Kingdom Brunel smoke every day?

    a. Seventy.
    b. Twenty.
    c. Forty.

9. What is 'Brunel's billiard table'?

10. In which cemetery (within engine-whistle range of Paddington Station) is Brunel buried?

11. *The Oxford Companion to British Railway History* speaks of 'the great triumvirate' of mid-nineteenth-century engineers. Two of them were Isambard Kingdom Brunel and Robert Stephenson, but who was the third?

    a. Daniel Gooch.
    b. Joseph Locke.
    c. John Fowler.

12. This statue is on the forecourt or 'piazza' of Euston Station (or it was, until recently put into temporary storage as construction work is carried on). Whom does it depict?

13.   … And why?

14.   Where was the statue originally located?

15.   What was 'Fowler's Ghost'?

16.   Which advocate of 'self-help' wrote the five-volume *Lives of the Engineers*, a very sycophantic work of 1862?

17.   This is George Leeman, who succeeded George Hudson as chairman of the York, Newcastle & Berwick Railway, and uncovered his shady dealings. Leeman was MP for York between 1865 and 1868 and highly regarded in the city. On which road in York does this statue stand?

18. Supply the surname of this eminent railway personage: George Mortimer —.

19. Which railway magnate built this?

20. What did this man (see below) invent? He stands near the Bank of England and, more relevantly for our purposes, Bank Underground station.

21. Which London Underground line used to be referred to by some people (including John Betjeman) as 'the Whittaker Wright line', Wright being its original financier?

22. At the beginning of the film *The Flying Scotsman* (1929), there appears the following notice: 'For the purposes of the film dramatic licence has been taken in regard to the safety equipment used on *The Flying Scotsman*.' Who had insisted on this?

23. In what sort of business was Wenman Joseph Bassett-Lowke primarily involved?

24. Who was 'Concrete Bob'? He founded a construction firm that is well-known today, and carries his name.

25. What was bizarre about the death of George Jackson Churchward, who had been Chief Mechanical Engineer of the Great Western?

26. In 1949, after he retired as Chief Mechanical Engineer of the Southern Railway, Oliver Bulleid became the Chief Mechanical Engineer of Irish Railways for which he built a locomotive that ran on – what? (It seems logical, given the location.)

27. In 1963, Alan Pegler made a purchase that would lead to his bankruptcy and his taking cheap lodgings above a chip shop near Paddington Station while seeking work as an actor. What did he buy? (It cost £3,000.)

28. Which founder of a modern train operating company was ordained by the Universal Life Church Monastery?

29. Which founder of a modern train operating company wrote a book called *Screw It, Let's Do It*?

30. Which sometime songwriter and record producer for Kylie Minogue revived the name of London & North Western Railway for various railway ventures, including a rolling stock maintenance company that is now (having been sold) Arriva Traincare?

31. Which transport group – formerly the operator of East Midlands Trains and South West Trains – was founded by Brian Souter and his sister, Ann Gloag?

32. Chris Donald was the founding editor of a successful comic publication. He is also a rail enthusiast, and he put some of the profits from his publication towards the revival of the Alnwick branch line in Northumberland, which ran from Alnmouth on the East Coast Main Line to Alnwick 3 miles away. What was the publication?

CELEBRITIES

33. When did Queen Victoria make her first railway journey?

    a. 1831.
    b. 1836.
    c. 1842.

34. The trains on which Queen Victoria travelled were preceded by a pilot train, and no trains were allowed to pass in the opposite direction except for ... what sort of trains?

35. Of which painting by J. M. W. Turner (first exhibited in 1844) did *The Oxford Companion to British Railway History* write that it 'not only demonstrates a mastery of chiaroscuro but reflects an ambivalence between the sublime past and infernal future: it was decades ahead of its time and pointed clearly towards Impressionism and Abstract Expressionism'?

36. Which famous American toured Britain by rail in 1902, 1903 and 1904?

37. Which author and war hero left the manuscript of a 250,000-word book at Reading Station waiting room in 1919, requiring him to write the whole thing again?

38. Which member of the cast of *Dad's Army* wrote, in 1923, a successful play (later filmed several times) called *The Ghost Train*?

39. Not hard to spot the artist in this photograph. It's Eric Gill. The photograph shows something he supplied to the London & North Eastern Railway, in return for which he received (apart from money) a ride on the footplate of the *Flying Scotsman*. What was it?

40. Who voiced the station announcements in the film *Brief Encounter*?

41. Paul McCartney recalled that, early in their acquaintance, he and John Lennon tried to write a 'bluesy, freight train song' along the lines of 'Midnight Special' or 'Rock Island Line'. What was the result?

42. Who met at Dartford railway station on 17 October 1961, with important consequences for the 1960s?

43. Which actress, best known for appearing in *Carry On* films, grew up in the station house at Laindon in Essex, her father being the station master?

44. In 1966, Dora Bryan starred in a film with the word 'Train' in the title, playing a headmistress. What was the film?

45. Which knighted actor led a successful campaign in 1969 to restore kippers to the menu of *The Brighton Belle*?

46. Which cricket commentator assisted the railway preservationists who, in the early 1970s, began a campaign that would lead to the reopening of part of the Alton–Winchester line as the Mid-Hants Railway?

47. Who was the lead singer of the group, Trainspotters, who had a hit (nearly) in 1971 with 'High Rise'? He is also a former Radio One DJ.

48. Which presenter of TV history programmes (with the accent on architecture) founded the Euston Arch Trust in 1996 with the aim of restoring the Arch?

49. What do Rod Stewart, Hughie Green, Winston Churchill, Phil Collins, Roger Daltrey, Eddie Izzard and Anne Diamond have in common?

50. In 1970, a British singer-songwriter released his third album. Its title suggested the railways of the Old (or Wild) West, and the image on the record sleeve suggested a station of that time and place, but the station depicted was actually Horsted Keynes on the preserved Bluebell Railway. Who was the singer-songwriter?

51. Which railway-themed song of 1980, performed by Sheena Easton, was among John Peel's all-time favourite singles?

52. For which railway-related activity was Terence Cuneo well known?

53. Which comedian is commemorated with a plaque at Mornington Crescent Station?

54. Which British record label arranged a tour by train for some of its artists in 1978?

55. Which *Great British Bake-off* judge once served on the BR Board?

56. Which BBC news presenter has written of her love of *The Caledonian Sleeper*, which she uses regularly?

57. Which *Antiques Roadshow* regular has written many books about railways, and used to live in a 1903 Great Western railway carriage (or at least, in a house to which such a carriage was attached)?

58. *Paul Merton's Secret Stations* was a TV series about which type of small, out-of-the-way station? (There are about 150 of them on the UK network.)

59. Which comedian's most famous routine was called 'This train don't stop Camborne Wednesdays'?

CRIMINALS AND CRIME

60. Which class of criminal is described here?

> They often visit the various railway stations and are
> generally smartly dressed as they linger there – some of
> them better than others. Some of the females are dressed
> like shopkeepers' wives, others like milliners, varying
> from nineteen to forty years of age, mostly from nineteen
> to twenty-five; some of them attired in cotton gowns,
> others in silks and satins.

61. Every September from 1856, the South Eastern Railway ran
special trains from London to rural Kent for a certain class of
worker. According to *The Oxford Companion to British Railway
History*, 'The trains began leaving London Bridge in the early
hours of the morning, and were notorious for violence and
drunkenness among passengers; in 1863, for instance, the
mayoress of Maidstone was assaulted on the platform.' Which
kind of worker?

62. What did Canon Victor L. Whitechurch have to do with
railway crime?

63. Which builder of Underground railways in London had
served time in the Eastern State Penitentiary, Philadelphia?

64. Which English prison, modelled on the above, and no longer used as a prison, is visible from a British main-line train?

65. Which comic opera features the following lyric?

> The idiot who, in railway carriages,
> scribbles on window panes,
> We only suffer
> To ride on a buffer
> In Parliamentary trains.

66. How many murders were committed in railway carriages between 1830 and 1914? Answers two either way acceptable.

67. Name any one of the murderers.

68. What are (or were) Müller lights?

69. About which of her own novels did Agatha Christie write, 'Each time I read it again, I think it commonplace, full of cliches, with an uninteresting plot. Many people, I am sorry to say, like it'?

70. Why did Brighton Station's left luggage office become notorious in 1934?

71. In 1955, a Mr Dean of Southend was in a non-smoking compartment of a train going from Upminster to Shoeburyness. When another man in the compartment lit a cigarette, Mr Dean pulled the communication cord to stop the train. What happened to Mr Dean as a result?

   a. He was prosecuted for improper use of the communication cord, but found not guilty on the grounds that it was better to have stopped the train than confront the smoker directly, which might have resulted in a fight.
   b. He received a letter from the General Manager of British Railways' Eastern Region congratulating him on his public spiritedness.
   c. He was prosecuted for improper use of the communication cord, found guilty and fined.

72. Which Conservative transport minister fled to France, to escape prosecution for tax fraud?

73. The line between Grantham and Skegness has an alternative title, incorporating the name of a type of rural criminal. What is it?

74. What crime occurred in a school sports hall in Market Deeping in May 2019?

CRITICS AND SATIRISTS

75. Who wrote the following:

> Proud were ye, Mountains, when in times of old,
> Your patriot sons, to stem invasive war,
> Intrenched your brows; ye gloried in the each scar;
> Now, for your shame, a Power, the Thirst of Gold,
> That rules o'er Britain like a baleful star,
> Wills that your peace, your beauty, shall be sold,
> And clear way made for her triumphal car.

76. Which Dickensian character said, 'Them confugion steamers … has done more to throw us out of our reg'lar work and bring ewents on at times when nobody counted on (especially them screeching railroad ones), than all the other frights that was ever took'?

77. Which other Dickensian character said, 'I con-sider that the rail is unconstitootional and an inwaser o' priwileges'?

78. Which well-known Victorian novelist wrote a book called *Rambles Beyond Railways*, which was published in 1851?

79. Which constitutional historian wrote, 'Every railway takes trade from the little town to the big town, because it enables the customer to buy in the big town'?

80. Which art critic and polymath (pictured above) said, in 1887, 'Railroads … are to me the loathsomest form of devilry now extant and deliberate, destructions of all wise social habit or possible natural beauty, carriages of damned souls on the ridges of their own graves'?

81. From which comic novel of 1889 is the following taken? 'So we went to the high-level platform and saw the engine driver, and asked him if he was going to Kingston. He said he couldn't say for certain, of course, but he rather thought he was.'

82. And what is the station concerned?

83. During the First World War, Britain's railways had been brought under state control and run by the Railway Executive Committee, a regime deemed more successful than the previous cut-throat competition between private companies. Nationalisation might have been made permanent after the war, but a major historical event swayed opinion against it. What was the event? (It occurred abroad.)

84. Which humorous book, by William Heath Robinson, begins: 'The Great Western Railway celebrates its one hundredth birthday this year, but unlike other centenarians such as trees and turtles, grows more youthful after a century of existence.' It was published in 1935, with an alliterative two-word title; the first word was 'Railway'; the second word was longer than the first by one letter.

85. David Croft, who co-wrote *Dad's Army*, *Hi-De-Hi* and *Are You Being Served?*, also co-wrote a sitcom set on a branch line threatened with closure. Name the sitcom.

86. In which publication is the railway correspondent called Dr B. Ching?

87. In 2003, a play satirising railway privatisation appeared in London. It was called *The Permanent Way*, and it was by a prolific left-wing playwright. Who?

ENTHUSIASTS

88. Who, on seeing a train pass through the countryside near Rugby, said, 'I rejoice to see it, and think that feudality is gone for ever'?

89. The first editor of the *Railway Magazine*, on its foundation in 1897, was George Augustus Sekon. That was a pen name. What was the real last name of Sekon (who was a witty man)?

90. The Railway Club, founded in 1899, was the first society for railway enthusiasts. When did it fold? Answers five years each way acceptable.

91. Which society of enthusiasts (initials MRC) occupies premises at 4 Calshot Street, London N1?

92. E. Beal practised a certain form of railway enthusiasm. In a book of 1937, he commended it with a quote from O. Henry: 'To be really happy in this world, you must have a little country where you don't live.' Which form of railway enthusiasm was he referring to?

93. Who wrote *The Trains We Loved*?

94. Supply the surnames of these well-known railway authors:

    O. S.
    L. T. C.
    Cecil J.

95. Who, before trainspotters, were the original 'spotters'?

96. What is the RCTS?

97. What word, according to Alan A. Jackson, compiler of *The Railway Dictionary*, denotes 'the most fanatical and extreme type of railway enthusiast'?

98. What is 'track bashing' (also known as 'buffer kissing')?

99. What, for a trainspotter, is a 'cop'?

100. Two of the following are terms of approval that might be used by fans of diesel traction on, for example, inhaling the oily reek of a passing Class 37; the other is not. Which is the imposter?

    a. Dreadful!
    b. Howling!
    c. Hellfire!

101. What does it mean to 'bunk a shed'?

102. By what title is Mark Smith better known? (It is also the name of his railway information website.)

103. The Tunbridge Wells–Eridge Railway Preservation Society was founded in 1985 to reopen that line, which is now the heritage Spa Valley Railway. By what potentially insulting, but actually self-deprecating, name was the Society widely known?

104. Nicholas Whittaker wrote a book about trainspotting, first published in 1995. It has a punning two-word title, the first word being 'Platform'. What is the title?

105. By what formerly futuristic name was the Campaign for Better Transport originally known?

106. After which comedian, writer, TV presenter, actor and transport campaigner were Virgin Voyager unit 22130 and National Express East Anglia Class 153 unit 153335 both named?

107. Who wrote, among about fifteen railway titles, *Fire and Steam: A new History of the Railways in Britain*; *On the Wrong Line: How Ideology and Incompetence Wrecked Britain's Railways*; *The Subterranean Railway*?

STAFF

108. What was a railwayman's 'bait'?

109. 'Little and often' is a footplate maxim. To what does it refer?

110. What did it mean for a footplate crew to be riding 'on the cushions'?

111. What railway job title was inherited from that of the armed men who travelled on mail coaches in the late eighteenth century?

112. Why did drivers and firemen on the early Metropolitan Railway tend to have beards?

113. Any train driver called 'a Captain Hornblower' had what characteristic?

114. Which humorous Victorian novel (ostensibly for children) contains the following lines? 'The man that drives the engine. Why, his smoke alone is worth a thousand pounds a puff.'

115. Parkeston Quay station at Harwich was opened in 1883. It was named after C. H. Parkes, who was chairman of which railway company?

116. Here is a jocose passage from a well-known early book on railways, *Our Iron Roads*, by F. S. Williams (1884). 'Botanists would have to go to Rothwell Haigh to find one solitary Fearn, and the florist would be delighted to find at Draycott a full-blown Rose each day, whilst a Marigold is perpetually blooming at Wolverhampton.' What does this have to do with railway staff?

117. A fireman on which type of train is commemorated in the following lines, written by Horatio Brown in 1891? (The date is significant.)

> So! I shall never see you more,
> You mighty lord of railway roar;
> The splendid stroke of driving-wheel,
> The burnished brass, the shining steel,
> Triumphant pride in him who drives
> From Paddington to far St Ives.
> Another year, and then your place
> Knows you no more; a pigmy race
> Usurps the glory of the road,
> And trails along a lesser load.

118. Station masters of the Great Western Railway favoured a certain sartorial adornment called 'engaging' by the *Oxford Companion to British Railway History*. What was it?

119. Where is this?

120. … And when? (Answers two years either way acceptable.)

121. What did railway workers do in 1911, 1919 and 1926?

122. What did drivers and firemen have in common with signalmen, messengers, carters and clerks?

123. The writer of a London & North Western Railway guidebook wrote that the people of a certain town 'have a railway look'. Which town?

124. Sir Lowthian Bell, who was deputy chairman of the North Eastern Railway between 1895 and 1904, had a famous granddaughter. Who was she?

125. In *The Wind in the Willows*, what does the engine driver ask Toad to do in return for a free ride?

126. A wheeltapper tapped wheels with a metal hammer. Why?

127. What was a railwayman's 'snap'?

128. What role was performed by a member of station staff informally referred to as a 'zookeeper'?

129. In railway slang what was a 'banjo player'?

130. And what was 'the Big Penny'?

131. Which professional football team originally comprised staff at the Carriage and Wagon Department of the Lancashire & Yorkshire Railway?

132. In 1925 John Elliot, who had been a journalist, joined the Southern Railway. Sir Herbert Walker, General Manager of the Southern, asked Elliot what job title he would like. Elliot suggested a title he'd heard used in America, and Walker agreed, 'because no-one will understand what it means and none of my railway officers will be upset'. What was it?

133. Who is this?

134. Which draughtsman, intermittently employed by London Transport in the 1920s, created the Tube Map, which was adopted in 1933?

135. In 1938, Sir Nigel Gresley's streamliner for the London & North Eastern Railway, *Mallard*, hit 126 mph on the East Coast Main Line, setting the world speed record for steam locomotives. The driver was Joseph Duddington, whose father and two brothers were also train drivers. What was unusual about Joe Duddington's dress sense?

136. About how many people worked on BR in 1948?

    a. 690,000.
    b. 390,000.
    c. 990,000.

137. About how many people work on the railways today?

    a. 190,000.
    b. 50,000.
    c. 110,000.

138. In 1948, about how many porters (goods and passenger) worked on BR?

    a. About 25,000.
    b. About 53,000.
    c. About 120,000.

139. What did BR call porters from the 1970s onwards?

140. When did railway staff officially cease to be 'servants'?

141. For what unfortunate reason does the name of train driver Jack Mills live on?

142. Here is a steam engine footplate. What is the name of the long down-pointing handle (the one terminating just to the left of the billy can)?

    a. The steam brake.
    b. The reverser.
    c. The regulator.

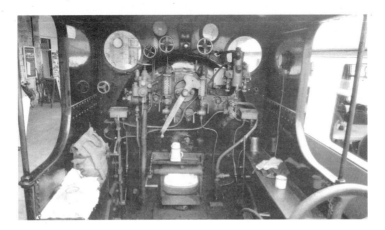

143. Which chairman of British Rail would ask for 'a box of good Havana cigars' rather than cash when undertaking a speaking engagement?

144. *Who's Who in Britain's Rail Industry* was published in 1982 and edited by E. L. Cornwell. It contains about 1,000 entries. How many are women?

    a. None.
    b. One.
    c. Four.

145. Two successive British Rail chairmen had the same name. What was it? (The initials spelt 'BR'.)

146. What does a motorman drive?

147. In 1991, during a radio BBC radio interview with James Naughtie, Terry Worrall, BR's Director of Operations, said, 'We are having problems with the type of snow, which is rare in the UK.' How was this summarised in modern folklore?

148. In 2004, on *Just a Minute*, Gyles Brandreth joked that as a boy he'd been under the impression that a well-known Latin tag meant, 'My dad's an engine driver'. Which one?

CHILDREN

149. Which engineer of railways accidentally swallowed a half-sovereign coin in 1843 while performing a magic trick for children?

150. Who were 'the Railway Children'? I mean, what were the names (first names will do) of the children in the novel by E. Nesbit?

151. Name any two of the three actors who played them in the film of 1970.

152. In *Railways and the Victorian Imagination*, Michael Freeman identifies a department store in Holborn, London, as 'Britain's most famous retailer of toy trains'. Its catalogue of 1906 had 'some 150 types available'. What was its name?

153. *The Wonder Book of Railways for Boys and Girls* was first published in 1911. How many editions had it gone through by 1950?

     a. Thirty-nine.
     b. Seven.
     c. Twenty-one.

154. Who was 'Uncle Allen'?

155. In the small hours of 13 October 1928, the Leeds–Bristol night mail (which carried passengers) collided with an empty goods train at Charfield in Gloucestershire. Gas cylinders on the night mail exploded and a fire broke out. Sixteen fatalities occurred. In his book *Red For Danger*, L. T. C. Rolt wrote that 'There was one strange and poignant feature of the Charfield disaster.' What was it?

156. With what type of railway location is the comic book character Alf Tupper ('the Tough of the Track') associated?

157. Rail Riders, formed in 1981, was (I quote from an advert) 'British Rail's exciting club for 5- to 15-year-olds'. It also called itself 'the happiest club in the land'. Which children's TV presenter promoted it?

158. In 1974, Elizabeth Beresford's children's book *The Secret Railway* was published. (It was about a preserved railway.) For which series of children's books is Beresford chiefly known?

159. *The Flockton Flyer* (1977–78) was a children's TV series about a preserved railway. Why did rail fans complain about the title?

160. Up to two children accompanied by an adult may travel free on British trains if they are of what age or below?

    a. Three.
    b. Four.
    c. Five.

161. Which railway-themed animation series for children was set in 'the top left-hand corner of Wales'?

162. Which modern-day train operator has revived Enid Blyton's Famous Five characters to promote its business in posters, TV and cinema adverts and a book?

POLITICIANS

163. Fill in the missing politician's name: 'Pitt is to A--------
     as London is to Paddington.'

164. Which politician first suggested that the railways might be
     nationalised?

165. Which railway was promoted by Charles Pearson (solicitor to
     the Corporation of London, and MP for Lambeth)?

166. Smoking was banned on most of the early railways, at least
     in theory. But the position changed in 1868 with the passing
     of a Regulation of Railways Act, which contained a clause
     requiring a smoking carriage to be attached to every train
     containing more than one carriage of the same class. Which
     Victorian philosopher and Liberal MP – sometimes described
     as a 'libertarian' – argued for it?

167. Which early-twentieth-century prime minister's father was a
     director of the North British Railway who made a fortune by
     railway speculations, fathered eight children and died in 1856
     aged thirty-six?

168. Who was the last British prime minister who never flew?

169. Which entrepreneur and Conservative MP for Everton (in the early 1930s) reduced (according to Oliver Wainright, in a *Guardian* article of 2013) 'the entire world to something that can fit in a box'.

170. She was Secretary of State for Transport between 1965 and 1968. Who was she?

171. Which cabinet minister under Margaret Thatcher had a grandfather who'd been chairman of the London & North Eastern Railway?

172. The Keighley & Worth Valley Railway Preservation Society was founded in 1962. Its first chairman would go on to be the Labour MP for Keighley. Who was he?

173. And which other former Labour MP for Keighley is the current Chair of the Keighley & Worth Valley Railway (as of 2022)?

174. Which 'Jimmy' was the last general secretary of the National Union of Railwaymen?

175. Michael Portillo was once the Secretary of State for Transport: true or false?

ANIMALS

176. Where is this?

177. The working timetables of the Great Western Railway enjoined the company's drivers to watch out for what during the hunting season?

178. The Great Northern Railway used to close its Doncaster works during a certain week of September to allow staff to attend a certain sporting event (or to forestall mass absenteeism). Name the event.

179. What is the name of T. S. Eliot's 'Railway Cat'?

180. With what sort of livestock did 'convoyers' have to do?

181. How many horses were in railway harness at the foundation of BR in 1947?

    a. 9,000.
    b. 4,000.
    c. 20,000.

182. Britain's last railway horse was retired on 21 February 1967. What was its name?

    a. Charlie.
    b. Mary.
    c. Champion.

183. In the late 1960s, the Tri-ang Hornby toy company produced a novelty model railway wagon in which an animal was carried. The wagon worked in conjunction with a track catch and a tunnel. As the wagon approached the tunnel, the track catch caused the animal's head to duck down just in time to avoid decapitation. What was the animal?

184. What, according to *The Railway and Steam Enthusiasts' Handbook* of 1973, were 'monkey specials'?

185. In 1982, the London Fat Cat competition was won by Tiddles, who weighed 30 lb. In which station, more commonly associated with another animal, did Tiddles live?

186. How many dogs can be taken on a British train without charge?

187. Which animal in a book by Henry Williamson has given its name to a railway line?

188. Which stop-frame animation film of 1993 features a dog and a penguin in a model railway chase?

189. In 2003, the Tay Bridge was refurbished. How many tons of bird faeces were scraped off?

    a. 10 tons.
    b. 100 tons.
    c. 1,000 tons.

190. Which bird caused controversy in relation to the statue of Sir Nigel Gresley unveiled at King's Cross in 2016?

TOPOGRAPHY

THE PERMANENT WAY

(RAILWAY TRACK AND ASSOCIATED FEATURES)

191. What is the name for the broken stone on which railway sleepers rest?

192. Define 'gauge'.

193. What was the broad gauge of the old Great Western (the distance between the rails, I mean)? Exactitude is required.

194. What did the broad-gauge Great Western call standard gauge?

195. The gauge of the Welsh Highland and Ffestiniog Railways is two foot. True or false?

196. How many sleepers are used in one mile of track?

    a. 2,112.
    b. 1,112.
    c. 612.

197. In 1830 there were fewer than 100 miles of public railways in Britain. What was the total, to the nearest thousand, in 1850?

198. What is 'the rule of the road' on Britain's railways?

199. Which regular lineside event did Charles Dickens describe as 'a shave in the air'?

200. In Charles Dickens' novel *Hard Times*, what seems to Mrs Sparsit to be creating 'a colossal strip of music-paper out of the evening sky'?

201. By what name are these London Underground lines collectively known: Circle, Metropolitan, District, Hammersmith & City?

202. What, on London Underground, is 'the neggy'?

203. What is 'tamping'?

204. In railway terms, what is the difference between up and down?

205. Of whom did Sherlock Holmes say that he 'has his rails and he runs on them'?

206. The following are the component parts of what? Arrival sidings; main yard; departure sidings.

207. What, in railway terms, was a hump?

208. After the Railway Grouping, three of the Big Four adopted upper-quadrant signalling; the GWR adopted lower-quadrant. What's the difference?

209. Which gradient helped *Mallard* achieve its speed record in 1938?

210. On which scenic railway route is 'the Long Drag' located?

211. Of what did O. S. Nock write, in *The Railway Enthusiast's Encyclopedia*: 'This incline has caused a locomotive problem throughout its existence, due to the very heavy traffic conveyed over the route'?

212. Which gradient is referred to in W. H. Auden's poem 'Night Mail'?

213. Where is the length of line known as 'the Sea Wall'?

214. Dr Beeching's report of 1963, *The Reshaping of British Railways*, recommended the closure of roughly what proportion of the network?

    a. A third.
    b. A quarter.
    c. A half.

215. What is the highest point reached by any British train? (It's in Wales, and it's at the top of a mountain.)

216. The Dollis Brook Viaduct is the highest point on which railway network?

217. The 'W' (below) is an instruction to the driver. What does it stand for?

218. Which prime minister said, 'You and I go by road or rail, but economists travel on infrastructure.'

219. It is contended by people who are pro-rail and anti-car that, while roads receive what is designated 'investment', railways receive ... what?

PARTICULAR RAILWAY LINES AND COMPANIES

220. Where was (and is) the Middleton Railway?

221. Shildon, in County Durham, grew from a village to a town when which railway company established its works there?

222. The Liverpool–Manchester Railway of 1830 scored a number of 'firsts'. Name any two of them.

223. What is the historical distinction of the London & Greenwich Railway, which opened in 1836?

224. What action by the Newcastle & Carlisle Railway in 1841 provoked warnings that its passengers were destined for hell?

225. The Newmarket & Chesterford Railway, which ran from Newmarket and Six Mile Bottom, existed between 1848 and 1851. Why is it sometimes said to be historically significant?

226. The last main line to reach London opened in 1899, with its terminus at Marylebone. Was the company concerned called the Grand Central Railway or the Great Central Railway?

227. The Great Northern & Southern Railway: was it real or fictional?

228. Do you need to take the East Coast or West Coast Main Line to go from London to Glasgow?

229. The Midland & Great Northern Joint Railway had its locomotive works in an unlikely spot. Was it:

    a. Cromer.
    b. Melton Constable.
    c. Castle Bytham.

230. The Bideford, Westward Ho! & Appledore Railway was opened in north-west Devon between 1901 and 1917, when it was requisitioned by the War Office. Two things were unusual about it. Name one.

231. What was 'the Withered Arm'?

232. Which pre-Grouping company described itself as 'the Premier Line'? (And there was some justification to this, beyond mere boasting.)

233. G. H. F. Nichols was a journalist who wrote for the *London Evening News* under the byline 'Quex'. He named a railway (later a 'line') of the London Underground. Which one?

234 Which pre-Grouping railway offered 'the best way'?

    a. The Great Northern.
    b. The London & South Western Railway.
    c. The Midland.

235. Which parsimonious colonel engineered the following lines?

> The Kent & East Sussex Railway.
> The East Kent Light Railway.
> The Ashover Light Railway.
> The Rye & Camber Tramway.

236. Which of the 'Big Four' covered the largest area?

237. Fast-moving steam locomotives could collect water by lowering a scoop into a trough set between the rails. One of the Big Four companies had no water troughs. Which one?

238. Which railway was known as 'the Docker's Umbrella' or 'the Ovee'?

239. 'The Vikings Landing at St Ives' was a production of the Great Western Railway. What was it?

240. The Talyllyn Railway is usually taken to be the first example of which type of railway?

241. On which railway is this occurring?

242. Which preserved railway is based at Pickering?

243. At which Highland resort is the preserved Strathspey Railway based?

244. Name two of the three preserved railways based at Porthmadog, Wales.

245. What became satirically known as 'the arrow of indecision' after its appearance in 1965?

246. Which Beatles film featured scenes shot on what is now the West Somerset Railway?

247. In 1983, BR sold off twenty-one of its twenty-three railway hotels. Two were retained for station reconstruction schemes; they were both in London. Name the hotels.

248. Also in 1983, BR sold the North British Hotel to the Forte Hotel Group who, after a refurbishment, reopened it as the New Balmoral Hotel. It stands 115 miles from Balmoral Castle, so why the name?

249. Britain has never had a maglev (magnetic levitation) railway. True or false?

250. Which line with an image problem was rebranded to become the chief component of Silverlink Metro in 1997?

251. The Elizabeth Line is part of London Underground. True or false?

STATIONS

252. What is the name given to the most basic and minimal type of railway station?

253. London has more main-line stations than any other city in the world. True or false?

254. In St Laurence's Churchyard in Reading, there's a memorial to a man killed on Reading Station in 1840 by a certain weather phenomenon. Which one?

255. Which London termini opened in the following years?

    1837.
    1838.
    1852.

256. Which British station has the most platforms?

257. Which London terminus has a lawn but no grass?

258. Which London terminus, opened in 1841 and rebuilt in 1854, featured the first station bookstall?

259. In which London station did WH Smith open its first station bookstall?

260. The design of which London terminus was inspired by the Imperial Riding School, Moscow?

261. What does Liverpool Street Station have to do with the man who was prime minister between 1812 and 1827?

262. Who painted Lordship Lane Station, Upper Norwood, in 1871?

263. Does Lordship Lane Station still exist?

264. In a children's book of 1876, *Discoveries and Inventions of the Nineteenth Century*, the Metropolitan Railway was discussed. Most of its stations, the child reader was informed, had 'roofs of the ordinary kind, open to the sky', but two stations were entirely underground, with roofs 'formed by the arches of brickwork immediately below the streets'. What were these stations? (One of them was subsequently renamed Euston Square.)

265. Glasgow used to have a station with a saint's name. Which one?

266. What type of platform is this?

267. Seven stations in Britain have, over time, been named after St James. Name any two of them.

268. Where is this?

269. In terms of station nomenclature, what do Sheffield, Nottingham, Manchester and London have in common?

270. How many railway stations does Pontefract have?

271. Which London terminus did John Betjeman compare to 'a branch public library in a Manchester suburb'?

272. Near which London terminus did Dr Watson once live?

273. Why was the lamp room at a railway station usually remotely located?

274. What is Britain's northernmost station?

275. This building, on Westminster Bridge Road near Waterloo, was once a private railway station. Two categories of passengers travelled on the trains that left from here, and one type of passenger could never speak to the other. What were these two types?

276. Which London Underground station was originally called Gillespie Road?

277. By 1895 an entrepreneur called George Jennings could boast of supplying the stations of thirty railway companies with public conveniences built to his up-to-date design. Name any one of the three new features of sanitary engineering he provided.

278. Where is this?

279. Which London terminus is referred to in these lines?

> Much tolerance and genial strength of mind
> Unbiased witnesses who wish to find
> This railway-station possible at all
> Must cheerfully expend. Artistical
> Ideas wither here: a magic power
> Alone can pardon and in pity dower
> With fictive charm a structure so immane.

280. In 1900, the trains of how many companies made scheduled stops at Carlisle Citadel Station?

    a. Three.
    b. Five.
    c. Seven.

281. Name any three of those companies.

282. Of which Scottish station does Simon Jenkins write, in *Britain's 100 Best Railway Stations*, 'This is one of the few stations that, in my opinion, qualify as a coherent work of art … The style is impossible to classify, variously called domestic revival, Queen Anne, arts-and-crafts and "chalet". To me, it also has a touch of Los Angeles Spanish'?

283. The roof of which London terminus collapsed on 5 December 1905?

284. In 1930, the LNER fitted a bench to the front of a slow-moving locomotive in order to expedite what process? (It was done in summer.)

285. Britain's first cylindrical railway station was on the London Underground. Where?

286. What did Waterloo Station have between 1934 and 1970, and London Victoria Station between 1933 and 1981?

287. Which Southern Railway commuter station of 1937 was credited by Pevsner as being 'one of the first to acknowledge a modern style'? It is thought of as the archetypal commuter station in the archetypal commuter town.

288. Name the four railway stations on the standard Monopoly board.

289. Which station hotel (since demolished) was referred to in 'The Fire Sermon' section of *The Waste Land* by T. S. Eliot?

290. To which station-related phenomenon of London Underground history do the following figures apply?

> 177,500 in September 1940.
> 5,000 in 1942.
> 150,000 in 1944–45.

291. The Railway Executive Committee was revived for the Second World War. In which disused Piccadilly Line station did its officers shelter during bombing raids?

292. What was the name of the station in the film *Brief Encounter*?

293. What do the following London Underground stations have in common:

Chancery Lane, Pimlico, Regent's Park, Notting Hill Gate?

294. What is the name for this type of station sign?

295. Monkton Combe, on the Camerton and Limpley Stoke line, starred as the titular station in which railway comedy film of 1954?

296. Which station was featured in *Terminus*, John Schlesinger's celebrated documentary of 1961?

297. A BRUTE was often seen on British stations in BR days. What was it?

298. Which West London station hotel did Keith Richards describe as '*the* place to be every Sunday night' in 1963?

299. At which station did Paul Simon supposedly write 'Homeward Bound' in July 1965? The town was at the time in Lancashire (it's now in Cheshire); it's famous for its rugby league team and is generally about the last place you'd expect to find Paul Simon.

300. The title of John Wain's novel of 1967, *The Smaller Sky*, refers to a London railway station. Which one?

301. Manchester Central Station closed in 1969. What is it today?

302. A station west of Southampton and another on the Central Line of the London Underground share the same name. What is it?

303. A particularly large number of railway scenes in feature films – including *Billy Liar*, *The Ipcress File*, *A Hard Day's Night*, *The Day of the Triffids*, *The Thirty-Nine Steps* (1978 version) – have been shot at Marylebone. Why?

304. Which station does Marylebone stand in for in the above-mentioned 1978 version of *The Thirty-Nine Steps*?

305. New Holland Pier station in North Lincolnshire closed in 1981. Why?

306. What, in a station, is a valance?

307. Which two towns have stations with the following suffixes? (They're both in Yorkshire.)

    a. Forster Square and Exchange.
    b. Westgate and Kirkgate.

308. In 1982 a short play by Harold Pinter was performed at the National Theatre. It had the same name as a railway station. Which one?

309. Which London terminus features in the title of a film written by and starring Paul McCartney?

310. Snow Hill Station was opened in Birmingham in 1987. There had been two previous Snow Hill stations. Where were they?

311. Which London Underground station ceased to be part of the Jubilee Line when the Jubilee Line Extension was opened in 1999?

312. In which London terminus does a brass band play every Friday evening?

313. What is the only London Underground station whose name contains no letters from the word 'mackerel'?

314. In *Prescriptions of a Pox Doctor's Clerk*, Robert Robinson asked rhetorically, 'How could a car be named after a railway station nobody ever got out at?' Which station was he thinking of?

315. Nine railway stations in Britain are Grade One listed. Name any two.

316. What is the busiest railway station outside London?

317. In which London Underground station can this be seen? (The architect was Charles Holden; it is Grade Two listed, and a terminus.)

318. Name the only London terminus lacking a direct Tube connection.

319. Which station is the terminus of the Wherry Lines, the Bittern Line and the Breckland Line?

320. What is the busiest station in Cornwall?

321. Which London terminus has a garden on its roof?

322. Which station, recently rebuilt, was voted by *Country Life* readers, in 2003, the second-worst eyesore in Britain after wind turbines?

TUNNELS

323. Define a railway tunnel.

324. Roughly what percentage of British railway tunnels were built by the Victorians? Answers 10 per cent either way acceptable.

325. The Liverpool–Manchester Railway (of 1830) incorporated two tunnels. Were they the first British railway tunnels? Yes or no?

326. Which tunnel is this?

327. What is said to happen in the Box Tunnel, Wiltshire, every 9 April?

328. The Thames Tunnel, built by Marc Brunel (with assistance from his son, Isambard) opened in 1843, and became a railway tunnel twenty years later. What world 'first' did it score?

329. In which ghost story is there 'a black tunnel, in whose massive architecture there was a barbarous, depressing, and forbidding air'?

330. What does this 'house' in Leinster Gardens, Bayswater, London, have to do with railway tunnels?

331. In 1882 the 'wonderfully named' (according to Christian Wolmar) Submarine Continental Railway Company, an offshoot of the South Eastern Railway, began boring a tunnel from the cliffs between Folkestone and Dover, aiming for France. The digging of this projected Channel Tunnel stopped in 1883. Why?

332. Through which tunnel did trains begin running on 1 September 1886?

333. What is the longest railway tunnel in the UK?

334. What sort of tunnel is known as a 'pipe'?

335. Which two London Underground lines are entirely underground (at least as far as passenger services are concerned)?

336. What percentage of the London Underground is underground? Answers 5 per cent either way acceptable.

337. Which tunnel was known as 'the hole'?

338. How many Sugar Loaf Tunnels are there in the UK?

339. On top of which tunnel is Mrs Wilberforce's house supposedly located in *The Ladykillers*?

340. Which tunnel is this?

341. How many people died in the construction of the Channel Tunnel? (Answers two either way acceptable.)

342. The Sharpthorne Tunnel in West Sussex is the longest tunnel on a certain type of railway. What type?

343. How many operational railway tunnels are there in Norfolk?

344. How many operational railway tunnels are there in Yorkshire?

     a. Twelve.
     b. Twenty-two.
     c. Thirty-seven.

345. Shortly after the completion of the Channel Tunnel, a steam locomotive was driven 8 miles into it from the French end. Why?

BRIDGES

346. The Royal Border Bridge, by Robert Stephenson, carries the East Coast Main Line across the Tweed. Is the border between England and Scotland:

    a. Under the bridge.
    b. North of the bridge.
    c. South of the bridge?

347. How many viaducts are there on the Settle & Carlisle Line? Answers four either way are acceptable.

348. Which theatre is in a railway arch beneath the viaduct that carries trains into Charing Cross? Either its present or its former name will do.

349. A railway viaduct used to run across Ludgate Hill in the City of London, between what is, at the time of writing, a Co-op and a Leon restaurant. Why, in particular, was it considered an eyesore?

350. Which Thames railway bridge in central London was painted by Claude Monet?

351. Most trains approaching Newcastle Station from the south go over the King Edward VII Bridge. A passenger looking to their right from that bridge sees how many other bridges?

352. The Digswell Viaduct carries the East Coast Main Line over the river Mimram. Which town does the viaduct overlook?

353. The Forth Bridge was built bigger than strictly necessary in order to be as strong as possible, and so avoid the fate of the Tay Bridge. But did more people die during the construction of the Forth Bridge than during the Tay Bridge disaster? Yes or no?

354. In his book of 1951, *The East Coast Route*, George Dow discloses the number of years it takes to paint the Forth Bridge. How many?

355. In which North Yorkshire town is this viaduct located?

JUNCTIONS

356. What is notable in geographic terms about Georgemas Junction in Caithness?

357. What is the current name of the station opened in 1869 as Waterloo Junction?

358. The Tenway is a junction in which novel by Anthony Trollope?

359. And which real junction is the Tenway based on?

360. Here is a limerick entitled 'There Was an Old Man at a Junction.' Who wrote it?

> There was an Old Man at a Junction,
> Whose feelings were wrong with compunction,
> When they said, 'This train's gone!'
> He exclaimed 'How forlorn!'
> But remained on the rails of the junction.

361. Where was this?

362. In which county is Effingham Junction located?

363. How many platforms are there at Clapham Junction? Answers three either way acceptable.

364. In pre-Grouping days, Shaftholme Junction (which is just north of Doncaster on the East Coast Main Line) marked the end of one company's territory and the start of another's. Which two?

365. What is a flat crossing?

366. And near which station on the East Coast Main Line is the only one in England located? (It's where the ECML intersects with the Nottingham–Lincoln line.)

367. This was reputedly the 'biggest railway crossing in the world'.

Where was it?

368. Which British novelist wrote *Bhowani Junction*, a novel of Indian railway life, published in 1954?

369. Insofar as the junction in Squeeze's song 'Up the Junction' is anything other than metaphorical, which actual railway junction is implied?

ROLLING STOCK

FAMOUS TRAINS

370. What is considered to be the first named train to have run in the United Kingdom?

371. This picture shows which famous train about to depart?

372. When did the *Special Scotch Express* become the *Flying Scotsman*?

      a. 1899.
      b. 1924.
      c. 1938.

373. There was once a train called *The Flying Welshman*.
True or false?

374. Where did *The Pines Express* go from and to?

375. What was highly unusual about *The Harrovian*, which ran
between 1911 and 1932? (The proximity to London implied by
the name is relevant.)

376. The first non-stop run of the *Flying Scotsman* (London–
Edinburgh) took place in which year?

377. There was a footplate crew change halfway through. How was
this achieved?

378. In 1932, the GWR claimed that *The Cheltenham Spa Express* was
the fastest train in the world. By what, racier, name was it
informally known?

379. Which express train was introduced in 1937 by the LMS in
honour of the coronation of George VI?

380. What did the signature tune of the 1950s radio detective series,
Paul Temple, have to do with trains?

381. What do the following named trains have in common?

> *The Galloway Piper.*
> *The Green Arrow.*
> *The Bristol.*
> *The Lothian Piper.*

382. 'If you will imagine the Palace of Versailles pulled out on a string of sausages, and mounted on bogies, it was like that.' This was written by Keith Waterhouse, about which train?

383. Which one of these Belles never existed?

> *The Devon Belle.*
> *The Bristol Belle.*
> *The Bournemouth Belle.*
> *The Kentish Belle.*

384. Which named train had a headboard surmounted by a bishop's mitre?

385. What had two Class 43 power cars and between six and nine Mark 3 coaches?

386. Which new train with a fancy name was advertised by Virgin Trains in the following embarrassing terms?

> It's fast. It's crazy fast …
> It's technically a train. It's better than a train, though.
> It's like a train and a laser made a baby while on holiday in Japan.

387. What is the fastest train in Britain?

LOCOMOTIVES

388. *Locomotion Number 1*, built by George and Robert Stephenson, hauled the first train on the Stockton & Darlington Railway. How much did *Locomotive Number 1* weigh? Answers 2 tons either way acceptable.

389. One of the engines that competed in the locomotive trials at Rainhill in 1829 (held to decide on the motive power for the Liverpool–Manchester Railway) was called *Cycloped*. What was unusual about it?

390. Name any of the other four locomotives competing at the trials.

391. How much did a Great Western *King* Class locomotive weigh? Answers 20 tons either way acceptable.

392. What was the principal fuel used in British locomotives until about 1860?

393. What type of engine is this?

394. What was significant about the locomotive built in 1893 by James Holden of the Great Eastern Railway and called *Petrolia*?

395. This photograph was taken at King's Cross in 1927. It shows *Flying Scotsman* – then three years old – and a small replica in the form of an engine called *Typhoon*. For use on which railway was *Typhoon* built?

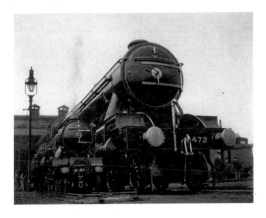

396. What was the name of the class to which locomotives called *Camelot*, *Tintagel*, *Excalibur* and *Merlin* belonged?

397. What type of tank engine is this?

      a. Pannier tank.
      b. Saddle tank.
      c. Side tank.

398. Which type of locomotive was bigger: an Atlantic or a Pacific?

399. Locomotives of the Great Northern Railway were manufactured and maintained at 'the Plant'. Where was this?

400. What is a 'light engine'?

401. What was an LMS Class 5 4-6-0 known as?

402. What is this engine doing?

403. Steam engines don't go 'backwards'. What do they do instead?

404. How many British locomotives were damaged in the Second World War? (Answers fifty either way acceptable.)

405. Many steam locomotives were given nicknames. Here are four of them:

Spam Cans.
Ironclads.
Spaceships.
Long Toms.

From this list, apply the right ones to the two engines pictured below.

406. In railway slang, what are 'blinkers'?

407. On 28 November 1942, Southern Railway Class D3 0-4-4T no. 2365 (a tank engine) was hauling a local train over Romney Marsh. A German fighter plane raked the engine and its carriages with bullets. What – in general terms – happened next?

408. Here is most of the first sentence of *The Three Railway Engines*, the first in the Reverend Wilbert Awdry's 'Railway Series' of books. Supply the final word.

'Once upon a time there was a little engine called —.'

409. What was the nickname given to this emblem, used on locomotives and other vehicles between 1948 and 1957?

410. In 1960, BR made its last steam locomotive. What was it called?

411. What was the name of the next main-line coal-fired steam locomotive to be built in Britain?

412. How many steam locomotives did BR have on 31 December 1960?

    a. 3,089.
    b. 7,009.
    c. 13,271.

413. What was wrong with Western Class diesel-hydraulic locomotive no. D1029, *Western Legionaire*?

414. Which type of big diesel was reputed to deafen its drivers?

415. How many locomotives were saved for preservation from the scrapyard at Barry Docks?

    a. 20.
    b. 195.
    c. 403.

UNITS

416. With what fruit was this vehicle associated?

417. What does DMU stand for?

418. The photograph below shows the first type of DMU made by BR. Trains like this were manufactured at the Derby works. What were they known as?

    a. Derby Doubles.
    b. Derby Diamonds.
    c. Derby Lightweights.

419. What is the name of the decorative feature on the DMU pictured above?

420. What was the world's only electric multiple-unit Pullman train?

421. Where is this?

422. What are Class 140, 141, 142, 143 and 144 diesel multiple units better known as?

CARRIAGES

423. What type of accommodation (broadly speaking) is this?

424. And what type of accommodation is this?

425. What did the Regulation of Railways Act 1844 do to improve travelling conditions for third-class passengers?

426. The Regulation of Railways Act of 1868 decreed a fine of how much for misuse of the communication cord? (The sum remained the same until 1977.)

427. When was it first possible to walk the full length of a passenger train? Answers ten years either way acceptable.

428. What type of roof does this carriage have?

429. What, in a railway carriage, is a droplight?

430. It may be cut, uncut or both; it is relatively warm in winter and cool in summer; it is hard to burn; its designers have included Enid Marx and Paul Nash. It begins with 'm'. What is it?

431. Most of the carriages on the *Flying Scotsman* train had compartments with corridors running along the side. The train was always marshalled so that the corridors were on which side (in terms of the compass)?

432. The high-speed *Coronation* train of the LNER had a 'beaver tail'. What is meant by this?

433. What was the fastest wooden vehicle ever to run on Britain's railways?

434. What faux-leather material – later found to be highly flammable – was frequently used on seats in inter-war smoking compartments?

435. What is a composite coach?

436. Which of the Big Four companies left its teak carriages unpainted?

437. In which year was the first cinema carriage introduced into regular service? Answers two years either way acceptable. (It showed films with sound.)

438. What is a slip coach?

439. Britain has never had double-decked carriages. True or false?

440. Which of the following statements is true?

> a. In the early 1970s, British Rail briefly operated a 'Disco Coach'; it was used on football specials on the East Coast Main Line and was decorated with graffiti tags.
> b. In the mid-1980s British Rail briefly operated a 'Kids' Coach' on the East Coast Main Line, incorporating a climbing frame, slide, padded floor, and an early video cassette player.

441. On the evening of Thursday, 30 August 1984, an HST ran from Paddington to Bristol Temple Meads at an average speed of 112.7 mph, the fastest diesel run between two major cities. A live transmission from a carriage of the train occurred during which BBC TV programme?

442. What, in railway slang, is a 'coffin'?

443. In which decade did train lavatories in Britain (on the national network) cease flushing directly onto the tracks?

444. Tube trains don't have air conditioning. True or false?

445. In which year did compartments disappear from the network?

> a. 1990.
> b. 2000.
> c. 2010.

446. On which two London Underground lines are there transverse as well as longitudinal seats? ('Transverse' means that you sit side-on to the window, rather than with your back to it.)

SLEEPERS, BOAT TRAINS AND CONTINENTAL SERVICES

447. When were proper sleeping carriages first introduced in Britain?

    a. 1845.
    b. 1873.
    c. 1890.

448. What was unusual about the sleeping car built in the 1870s by Sir Arthur Heywood for the railway that ran around his country estate at Duffield, Derbyshire?

449. In Britain it was called the International Sleeping Car Company. By which more familiar French name was this company known in Europe?

450. When was third-class sleeping accommodation first provided on British trains?

    a. 1876.
    b. 1896.
    c. 1928.

451. Into which sub-divisions did *Punch* propose that sleeping carriages be divided?

452. What was distinctive about the coat hangers provided in sleeping compartments on the LNER?

453. What were 'Ocean Specials'?

454. Which famous novelist made his breakthrough with a book published in 1932 and set aboard an international sleeper train?

455. Which British composer wrote the music for *Night Mail* (the documentary about the train of that name made by the GPO film unit in 1936) and had a night train named after him? (But when most people think of *Night Mail*, they think of the poem by Auden read out as the voiceover.)

456. Which London station was 'the Gateway to the Continent'?

457. *The Golden Arrow* was a luxury train running from London Victoria to Dover, where its passengers boarded a ferry (or steamer) for Calais. From Calais, the service continued to Paris on a train called what?

458. *The Night Ferry* service saw the carriages of a train from Victoria to Dover loaded onto a ferry and taken to Dunkirk, where they continued on to Paris. (Or vice versa.) In 1974, the Christmas special and final episode of which long-running British sitcom featured a son waving his father off on *The Night Ferry*? (And he is delighted to be rid of him.)

459. Ostensibly, *The Night Ferry* ran non-stop from Victoria to Dover, but it did once stop to pick up a VIP passenger – at Sevenoaks on 16 December 1951. The *Night Ferry* conductor had orders to put a bottle of Dewar's White Label Whisky, soda water and cracked ice in the compartment reserved for the guest. Who was this VIP?

460. What were the *vases de nuit* provided on *The Night Ferry*?

461. Why have there never been train ferries across the Irish Sea?

462. What was the brand name under which BR operated hovercrafts (if that is the plural) between 1965 and 1981? (The name implied swiftness.)

463. Where did *The Night Capitals* train go from and to?

464. Where did *The Night Limited* go from and to?

465. Which British novelist wrote, 'Suicide is the night train, speeding your way to darkness'?

466. Which ground-breaking train first ran in 1994?

467. How many international trains call at Stratford International Station every day?

FREIGHT

468. What were freight trains called in Britain until about 1960?

469. Which riverside London railway station, opened in 1838, closed to passengers in 1848 but continued as a goods station until its final closure in 1968?

470. Who is recorded, in a novel of 1897, as arranging the nocturnal delivery, by the Great Northern Railway, of fifty boxes of soil?

471. What was demurrage?

472. What, on BR, was a GUV?

473. This type of vehicle was often used by BR to make door-to-door deliveries. Its name incorporated that of a type of animal. What was it?

474. What was a 'pick-up goods'?

475. What was a 'steam banana'?

476. In 1897, railways were conveying to London what percentage of the city's milk consumption?

    a. 56 per cent.
    b. 76 per cent
    c. 96 per cent.

477. According to *The Oxford Companion to British Railway History*, which was higher between the 1860s and 1960s, freight revenue or passenger traffic revenue?

478. And how much less was freight revenue than passenger revenue in the early 1990s?

    a. Half.
    b. A quarter.
    c. A tenth.

479. *The Night Mail* (1923–93) was a TPO. What does that stand for?

480. Which BR parcels delivery service was advertised with the slogan, 'You've got a deadline. We've got a lifeline'?

BEING A PASSENGER

PASSENGERS IN GENERAL

481. According to *The Railway Traveller's Handy Book* (1862), three topics of conversation should be avoided by railway travellers. Name any one of them.

482. Which novelist found that 'after a few days' practice, I would write as quickly in a railway carriage as I could at my desk'?

483. Which British prime minister wrote, in 1870, 'I cannot read in a railroad, and the human voice is distressing to me amid the whirl and the whistling, and the wild panting of the loosened megatheria who drag us'?

484. 'One must always have something sensational to read in the train?' In which play is this line spoken?

485. In 'The Adventure of Silver Blaze', how did Sherlock Holmes pass the time on the train journey to Dartmoor?

486. You are on a train in the period between 1900 and the year of the Railway Grouping (1923) – any train you like except one operated by the South Eastern & Chatham Railway. You fancy lighting up. Do the signs guiding you on where this is allowable read 'Smoking' or 'Non-Smoking'?

487. In the 1920s, which predominated: Smoking carriages or Non-smoking carriages?

488. From about 1840, Ladies Only compartments began to appear on British trains. Were they ever mandatory?

489. When did Ladies Only compartments disappear from the network? Answers five years either way acceptable.

490. Were there ever Ladies Only smoking compartments?

491. Until the mid-twentieth century, station waiting rooms tended to be designated for men or women. Where they were not so designated, they usually shared a certain design characteristic. What was it?

492. What was inside ceramic or metal footwarmers? (There are two possible answers; either will do.)

493. The Great Northern Railway pioneered the use of footwarmers. In 1871, the company officially had 1,000 of them, but how many were missing presumed stolen?

    a. 16.
    b. 74.
    c. 359.

494. According to *The Traveller's Guide to Great Britain and Ireland* (1930) who, in a compartment, gets to decide whether the window should be open or closed?

495. Of which Big Four company is this sign characteristic?

496. When did the lyric beginning with the following two lines appear on posters in stations?

> Railways aren't allowed to say
> What delayed the trains today.

497. Who wrote the following lines?

> When, in a pause between the stations, quiet
> Descended on the carriage we would talk
> Loud gibberish in angry argument,
> Pretending to be foreign.

498. In which film (of 1963) does Tony Hancock play the bowler-hatted employee of United International Transatlantic Consolidated Amalgamation Limited? (Boarding a BR Southern Region electric commuter train, he sighingly contemplates 'journey number 6,833', before breaking free of his commute to become an Impressionist painter … Although his landlady says of his work, 'It doesn't impress me at all.')

499. Who wrote, in 1975, 'I sought trains; I found passengers'?

500. Which type of passenger is described here? 'The anti-hero of our age. More than the soldier, the nuclear physicist, the political prisoner or the starving child, he indicates where we've gone wrong.'

501. Which of the following is true of the smoking carriages on Tube trains?

    a. The seats were covered in a different-coloured moquette to those of non-smoking carriages.
    b. There were no ashtrays.
    c. They were always at the ends of trains.

502. In which year did a complete ban on smoking on the national railway network (stations and trains) come in? Answers within one year either side are acceptable.

TIMETABLES AND TIMES

503. *Bradshaw's General Railway & Steam Navigation Guide for Great Britain and Ireland* was the standard British railway timetable from 1842 to 1961, by which time it was being published alongside BR's own timetables. It was the brainchild of a man called Bradshaw. What was his first name?

504. What was the *ABC Guide*, and why was it so called?

505. 'Railway Time' was the same as Greenwich Time. True or false?

506. Which famous novelist (an American who lived mostly in Britain) sent this telegram? 'Will alight precipitately at 5.38 from the deliberate 1.50.' Note the verbosity.

507. Who waited for a train at Clapham Junction on 21 November 1895, between 2 p.m. and 2.30?

508. In which novel of 1911 does this passage occur?

> 'I wonder whether I can get on to Brighton tonight if I take the six train?' Hilda asked ...
>
> At the station the head porter received their inquiry for a *Bradshaw* with a dull stare and a shake of the head. No such thing had ever been asked for at Bursley Station before, and the man's imagination could not go beyond the soiled timetables loosely pinned and pasted up on the walls of the booking-office.

509. For a certain two minutes in 1919 every train in Britain either stopped or delayed its departure. Why?

510. Which of the following station clocks is the odd one out?

> Waterloo.
> Paddington.
> Victoria.
> Brighton.

511. What was a 'clockface' service?

512. Here is an amended quotation from a sentence in *The Railway Workers: 1840–1970*, by Frank McKenna: 'An engine-driver drew a — like a gunfighter drew a Colt.' Supply the missing word.

513. Who, in a comedy film of 1937, said, 'The next train's gone?'

514. G. K. Chesterton is reputed to have said that the only sure way of catching a train was to do what?

515. What are working timetables?

516. The title of which Agatha Christie novel incorporates a train time?

517. In what year did BR and London Transport adopt the 24-hour time system for their timetables? Answers two years either way acceptable.

518. What is the longest train journey available in the UK without changing?

519. What did an assistant at the WH Smith in Euston Station ask when the author of this book enquired as to whether they sold timetables?

CLASSES

520. Who said third-class accommodation was 'a breach of contract, a premium to the lower orders to go uselessly about the country'?

521. Early third-class railway carriages were often roofless and had no seats. Carriages of this type were nicknamed 'Stanhopes'. Why?

522. What was a 'Parliamentary Train'?

523. Which pre-Grouping company was the first to abolish second class?

524. In 1913, what percentage of journeys were made in Third Class?

     a. 51 per cent.
     b. 76 per cent.
     c. 96 per cent.

525. What was unique about Dr Watson's train journey to Little Purlington, undertaken in the Sherlock Holmes story, 'The Retired Colourman'?

526. There was originally a class system on the cut-and-cover lines of the London Underground: the Metropolitan and the District. When was it abolished? (Answers two years either way acceptable.)

527. In 1956, 'Third' became 'Second' to make the discrepancy seem less. But when did 'Second' give way to 'Standard'? Answers three years either way are acceptable.

528. Can a first-class passenger claim a refund if, owing to some operational emergency, First Class is thrown open to passengers from Third/Second/Standard?

TICKETS

529. What type of ticket is this? (It is named after its inventor.)

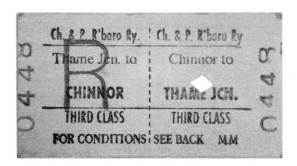

530. When did the above type of ticket disappear from BR? Answers three years either way acceptable.

531. Why might one of the above type of tickets have been snipped in half by a ticket clerk?

532. What is William Carson – known as 'Tickety Carson'– credited with having invented?

533. Why are booking offices so called?

534. Which line was nicknamed 'the Twopenny Tube'?

535. What is a privilege ticket?

536. What were travelling ticket inspectors informally known as during the 1970s? The name derives from the police.

537. What sort of passenger, on the London Underground of the late twentieth century, was a referred to as a 'Twirly'?

538. When was the Oyster card introduced on public transport in London?

    a. 1998.
    b. 2003.
    c. 2005.

REFRESHMENTS

539. When was the first dining car introduced? Answers within ten years either way are acceptable.

540. In the fairly well known Victorian railway joke, how (in general terms) does 'Boy' selling refreshments reply to the sceptical passenger's enquiry: 'Are the sandwiches fresh, boy?'

541. What, in another Victorian railway joke, does the manageress of a first-class station refreshment room ask her assistant to do with some cakes that have gone stale?

542. Which Victorian novelist called the railway sandwich 'the disgrace of England'?

543. Which station – which had an expensive railway refreshment room – was known to aggrieved passengers as 'Swindelum'?

544. Which august personage of the GWR wrote a letter to the manager of that refreshment room beginning, 'Dear Sir, I assure you Mr Player is wrong in supposing that I thought you purchased inferior coffee. I thought I said to him I was surprised that you should buy such bad roasted corn. I did not believe you had any such thing as coffee in the place; I am certain I never tasted any'?

545. Who wrote the short story of 1866 that begins, 'I am the boy at what is called the Refreshment Room at Mugby Junction, and what's proudest boast is that it never yet refreshed a mortal being ...'

546. What name was given to the following concoction of 1928?

> 2 oz blended Scotch whisky;
> 2 oz sweet vermouth;
> 1½ tsp sugar syrup;
> 1 tsp Angostura bitters;
> slice of lemon.

547. In which novel by Evelyn Waugh does this passage appear?

> The train was nearly empty. I had my suitcase put in the corner of a third-class carriage and took a seat in the dining car. 'First dinner after Reading, sir; about seven o'clock. Can I get you anything now?' I ordered gin and vermouth; it was brought to me as we pulled out of the station. The knives and forks set up their regular jingle; the bright landscape rolled past the windows.

548. How many Travellers-Fare Casey Jones burgers were sold by BR in 1983? A hundred thousand either way is fine.

549. Which pub advertises itself as 'the last pub before Paris'?

550. What is the maximum amount of alcohol a passenger is allowed to carry onto a Eurostar? Answers are required for wine, beer and spirits.

551. How many dining cars were there on the BR network in 1997?

    a. 25.

    b. 90.

    c. 250.

552. Which comedian said, 'I'm not a fan of the modern railway system. I strongly object to paying twenty-seven pounds fifty to walk the length of the train with a sausage in a plastic box'? (Her first name was also the name of a railway station.)

553. What, as of 2022, is the only national train operator to provide dining cars?

EROTICA

554. Which future engineer of railways, having been sent to Brighton in 1828 for recuperation after an accident, further undermined his health by 'exertions with actresses'?

555. Who did the actress Fanny Kemble describe, in a letter to a friend of 26 August 1830, as follows?

> Now for a word or two about the master of all these marvels, with whom I am most horribly in love. He is a man of from fifty to fifty-five years of age; his face is fine, though careworn, and bears an expression of deep thoughtfulness; his mode of explaining his ideas is peculiar and very original, striking, and forcible; and although his accent indicates strongly his north-country birth, his language has not the slightest touch of vulgarity or coarseness. He has certainly turned my head.

556. Which novel of 1836, which has a good deal to do with stagecoaches, has the following as an opening inscription to a chapter: 'The course of true love is not a railway'?

557. Which music hall star sang (from about 1895) 'What Did She Know About Railways?', a risqué song about a naïve young woman taking her first train journey?

558. What type of railway accommodation does *The Oxford Companion to British Railway History* describe (ironically) as 'convenient for sexual assaults'?

559. The builder of Underground railways, Charles Tyson Yerkes, arrived in London in 1898 aged sixty-one. He was accompanied by his mistress, Emilie Busbey Grigsby. How old was she?

    a. Seventeen.
    b. Twenty-one.
    c. Twenty-four.

560. From the 1860s until the early twentieth century, a very regular shuttle service used to run between two London main-line termini originally owned by the South Eastern Railway. The journey took about eight minutes, and the trains were of compartment stock. Consequently, they became places of assignation for prostitutes and their clients. What were the two termini?

561. This is Temple Mills railway sidings in East London in the 1950s – not, on the face of it, a very erotic photograph. But a few years before, Temple Mills was the setting of the violent climax to the torrid love story played out in a British film directed by Robert Hamer and starring Googie Withers, John McCallum and Jack Warner. What film?

562. At the end of Alfred Hitchcock's film, *North by Northwest* (1959), Cary Grant takes Eva Marie Saint into his upper sleeping berth in a Pullman railcar. The scene then changes to one suggestive of the sex act. What is that scene?

563. What was the name of the novel of 1959 by John Hadfield, dramatised by the BBC in 1994, about a man in a wheelchair (having lost his legs in a railway accident) who lives in a railway carriage on a doomed country branch line with his three nubile daughters?

564. Which future politician, born Shirley Caitlin, had an affair at Oxford University with the future BR chairman, Peter Parker?

ACCIDENTS

565. The first forty years of railways were littered with accidents, but what were your chances of being killed on the railways in 1845?

    a. About one in 60,000.
    b. About one in 150,000.
    c. About one in 420,000.

566. Here is a quotation from a letter written on 16 September 1830 by the Whig statesman, Henry Brougham. 'He has been killed by a steam carriage. The folly of 700 people going fifteen miles an hour, in six carriages on a narrow road, exceeds belief. But they have paid a heavy price.' Who had been killed?

567. Which novel, by Robert Louis Stevenson, contains a humorous account of a railway accident?

568. The manuscript of which novel was Charles Dickens carrying in his pocket when he was involved in the Staplehurst train crash in 1865? (It was one of his own.)

569. What happened on the fifth anniversary of the Staplehurst crash?

570. Which other successful novelist was involved in a train crash in 1999, and what was the crash?

571. This is North British Railways engine no. 224, photographed in 1880. What accident had it been involved in?

572. Britain's worst railway accident happened at Quintinshill, near Gretna Green, in 1915. How many people died? Answers twenty either way acceptable.

573. And how many trains were involved in the crash?

574. Arnold Bennett wrote a novel (of 1927) whose central event was a railway accident. It's one of his more obscure works, and it has a one-word title. What is it?

575. What does SPAD stand for?

576. The general manager of which railway said, of the Sevenoaks railway disaster of 1927 (in which thirteen people died), 'Accidents don't happen by accident.'

577. In which year was there an accident on this railway?

578. In railwaymen's slang what dangerous practice was known as 'Widows and Orphans'?

COLOUR SECTION

579. What colour is a despatch flag?

580. What colour was Stephenson's *Rocket*?

581. Which railway, nicknamed both the 'Slow & Dirty' and the 'Swift and Delightful', had locomotives of Prussian Blue?

582. From 1893, the London & South Western Railway issued all grades of staff with red neckties. Why red?

583. Here is a list of railway companies, followed by a list of shades of green. Match the company to the shade of green.

> Southern Railway.
> Great Western Railway.
> North British Railway.
> London, Brighton & South Coast Railway.
> London & North Eastern Railway.

> Brunswick Green.
> Improved Engine Green.
> Malachite Green.
> Apple Green.
> Bronze Green.

584. Why was the livery of Cambrian Railways known as 'Invisible Green'?

585. What colour were Pullman carriages (as operated in Britain)?

586. In his book *Station Colours*, Peter Smith describes one of the Big Four as 'the green railway'. Which one?

587. Which railway is known as 'the Clockwork Orange'?

588. In terms of BR carriage liveries, 'carmine and cream' is the same as 'blood and custard'. True or false?

589. 'Carmine and cream' is the same as 'plum and spilt milk'. True or false?

590. The record-breaking *Mallard* was what sort of blue?

     a. Garter Blue.
     b. Caledonian Blue.
     c. Marlborough Blue.

591. And its wheels were red, but of which shade?

     a. Venetian Red.
     b. New Vermilion.
     c. Indian Red.

592. With which two railway companies (one pre-, one post-Grouping) is the shade Crimson Lake associated?

593. Which railway company painted its stations in 'Light and Dark Stone'?

594. In the 1930s, Frank Pick, head of design (in effect) at London Transport, commissioned a series of seat moquettes from some leading designers, including Paul Nash and Enid Marx. The designers were advised to favour a certain colour, believed to lend a 'serene' atmosphere to carriage interiors. What was it?

595. What was this luxury BR diesel train of the 1960s called? The name incorporates a colour.

596. Which designer (whose surname was also a colour) devised Rail Blue as the engine and carriage livery of BR from 1965 onwards?

597. On some carriages, Rail Blue was matched with Pearl Grey. How was the combination commonly described by its deprecators?

598. What colour (externally) were the following Tube stocks?

> 1938 Stock.
> 1959 Stock.
> 1992 Stock.

599. What, on the modern railway, are the 'Yellow Trains'?

600. What is known as 'the Ginger Line'?

ANSWERS

PEOPLE (AND ANIMALS)

ENTREPRENEURS AND ENGINEERS

1. James Watt.

2. George was not only the father of Robert, he was also known as 'the father of British railways'.

3. They laughed. (At least, according to Tom Quinn, in *Railway's Strangest Tales*.)

4. *Blucher*.

5. Thomas Cook. After (sober) festivities at Loughborough, he urged the attendees to give 'one more cheer for Teetotalism and Railwayism'.

6. b. His yacht, *Titania*.

7. York.

8. c. Forty.

9. The very flat stretch of the Great Western Main Line between Paddington and Bristol. It enables high-speed running to the extent that the train always seems to be hurtling towards Paddington, though one's coffee barely trembles in the cup.

10. Kensal Green.

11. b. Joseph Locke. He had been articled to George Stephenson, but fell out with him over alignment errors in the two tunnels of the Liverpool–Manchester Railway. Locke was more cautious than the Stephensons. He favoured going around or over obstacles rather than through them, so he built fewer tunnels, but more steep gradients, as seen in his work on what became the West Coast Main Line in Scotland.

12. Robert Stephenson. The sculptor was Baron Carlo Marochetti.

13. Euston was the terminus of the London & Birmingham Railway (1837), which Robert Stephenson engineered.

14. Between the two stone lodges that survive (they are now pubs) and which mark the old Euston Road entrance to the station. The statue was moved to the piazza when the new Euston was built. A statue of George Stephenson, stood in the Great Hall of Euston Station, which was built in 1846, and has been described as 'the grandest waiting room in Britain'. This statue is now in the National Railway Museum.

15. John Fowler designed an experimental 'fireless' locomotive for use in the tunnels of the early Metropolitan Railway, of which he was the Chief Engineer. With heat retention by firebricks, and the use of re-condensing equipment, the release of smoke and steam was theoretically minimised. It didn't work, however, and after trial runs in 1861 and 1862 it was discarded. Fowler, embarrassed, never spoke of it, which is why in 1901 the *Railway Magazine* called it his 'ghost'.

16. Samuel Smiles, who claimed that George Stephenson had actually *invented* railways.

17. Leeman Road, formerly Station Road. Regarding Leeman's adversary ... Hudson Street in York had been named after George Hudson but was renamed Railway Street after Leeman had exposed him. In 1971, on the hundredth anniversary of Hudson's death, the street was renamed George Hudson Street.

18. Pullman. He was an American, but qualifies for this book by virtue of the fact that his luxury sleeping and dining carriages were used in Britain from 1 June 1874 (Bradford to London) by the Midland Railway.

19. Sir Edward Watkin, who in 1881 was a director of the Metropolitan Railway, the South Eastern Railway, the Manchester, Sheffield and Lincolnshire Railway, and six others. The photograph shows 'Watkin's Tower' in Wembley Park, which he created and opened in 1894 to lure people to Wembley Park Station on the Metropolitan Railway. The idea was to build a tower higher than the Eiffel, but the plan foundered, as did the tower, on marshy ground. It never progressed beyond the first stage and was demolished in 1907. Today, the site is occupied by Wembley Stadium.

20. The plaque beneath the statue reads,

J. H. GREATHEAD
CHIEF ENGINEER
CITY AND SOUTH LONDON RAILWAY
INVENTOR OF THE TRAVELLING SHIELD
THAT MADE POSSIBLE THE CUTTING
OF THE TUNNELS OF LONDON'S
DEEP LEVEL TUBE SYSTEM.

…which needs a slight gloss. The 'travelling shield' is more commonly known as a 'tunnelling shield'. It resembled a giant toilet roll that was projected through the London clay with men digging inside. The City & South London Railway was opened in 1890 running from Stockwell to King William Street, reaching Bank in 1900. Whether Greathead *really* invented the tunnelling shield is moot. It was perhaps a refinement of an excavating device invented by Marc Brunel to dig the Thames Tunnel between 1825 and 1843.

21. The Bakerloo Line. Wright's London Globe & Finance Corporation began excavating it in 1898, but in 1900 the company went bust. In 1904, after being sentenced to seven years' hard labour for fraud at the Old Bailey, Wright handed his gold watch to a friend, saying, 'I won't be needing this where I'm going'. He went into the Gentlemen's lavatory and swallowed a phial of prussic acid, with fatal results. It transpired that he also had a fully loaded revolver on him.

22. Nigel Gresley, Chief Mechanical Engineer of the London & North Eastern Railway. He was particularly indignant about the scene in which the heroine uncouples the engine from the moving train using a penknife.

23. The manufacture and retailing of model trains. 'Model trains' will do as an answer; 'toy trains' will not.

24. Robert McAlpine. By his pioneering use of concrete, he could get things done quickly. McAlpine, who started as a brickie's labourer, is best known for the Glenfinnan Viaduct on the West Highland Line, which is 416 yards long, with twenty-one arches. He founded the construction firm now known as Sir Robert McAlpine.

25. He was killed, in retirement, by a locomotive made by the company of which he had been the CME. It happened on 19 December 1933. Churchward continued to live in GWR accommodation at Swindon after his retirement, and he was walking along the main line in foggy weather when he spotted a defective sleeper. As he paused to inspect it, he was struck by the Paddington–Fishguard express, hauled by an engine of the Castle Class (designed by Charles Collett) which had evolved from Churchward's own Star Class. Churchward had developed a series of elegant, efficient and reliable engines with standardised components.

26. Peat, of which Eire had plenty, whereas it had almost no indigenous coal. The locomotive was trialled but never saw active service, being overtaken by dieselisation. It was scrapped in 1965.

27. *Flying Scotsman* locomotive.

28. Richard Branson. The Universal Life Church Monastery is a non-denominational online church that believes 'we are all children of the same universe'. Its aim is to ordain everyone. At the moment, it claims 20 million ministers.

29. Richard Branson.

30. Pete Waterman.

31. The Stagecoach Group.

32. *Viz* … which in 1987 introduced a character called Timothy Potter, Trainspotter. In 2003 Chris Donald wrote in *The Oldie* magazine, 'I believe that trainspotting was just one symptom of an underlying problem which, I fear, is with one to stay. Anoraxia, you might call it?' He had just been describing how he catalogues all his holiday snaps with seven-digit numbers. Part of the Alnwick branch is now operated as a preserved line by the Aln Valley Railway.

CELEBRITIES

33. c. 1842 – from Windsor to Paddington.

34. Mail trains.

35. *Rain, Steam and Speed – The Great Western Railway*.

36. Buffalo Bill.

37. T. E. Lawrence (Lawrence of Arabia). The book was *Seven Pillars of Wisdom*.

38. Arnold Ridley (Private Godfrey). He was inspired to write it during a long wait at Mangotsfield railway station, near Bristol, and he completed it in less than a week. He didn't like to talk about the play. He sold the rights to it in order to finance a film, and so did not benefit from its great success. He did, however, sometimes play the station master, Saul Hodgkin, in stage productions, in the earliest of which he had to be heavily made up to look older, whereas in the later ones (as he told the *Guardian* in 1976), 'I had a job making myself look young enough.' Ridley wrote another railway-themed play called *The Wrecker*. When Ridley appeared on *This Is Your Life*, he was accosted by Eamonn Andrews at Marylebone Station.

39. The Gill Sans typeface, as used on the headboard of the *Flying Scotsman* train. The one in the photograph was hand-painted by Gill.

40. Noel Coward, screenwriter of the film.

41. 'One After 909', written perhaps as early as 1957, and released in 1970 on *Let It Be*.

42. Mick Jagger and Keith Richards. They had been at primary school together but had then gone to different secondary schools. 'When Mick Jagger walked on to Platform 2 of Dartford Railway Station in October 1961,' writes David Hepworth in *A Fabulous Creation: How the LP Saved Our Lives*, 'the fact that he was carrying an import copy of *Rockin' at the Hops* with Chuck Berry's silhouette cut out on the cover was what attracted the eye of Keith Richards. This inevitably led to a conversation. The conversation resulted in the Rolling Stones.'

43. Joan Sims. There is a plaque to her memory at the station entrance.

44. *The Great St Trinian's Train Robbery.*

45. Laurence Olivier. On 24 March 1970, a man called Collie Cox wrote a letter to the *Daily Telegraph* about the matter, concluding, 'Not even when nightly strangling Desdemona at the National Theatre has Sir Laurence acted to a more noble purpose.'

46. John Arlott, who lived for a time in Alresford, a station on the line.

47. Mike Read.

48. Dan Cruickshank, who traced 60 per cent of the stones that had constituted the Arch to the bottom of the river Lea, where they were plugging a hole in the riverbed. The stones were salvaged in 2009. The Arch restored could yet become a landmark of the expanded version of Euston that will accommodate HS2. I once interviewed Cruickshank about the Arch (which, strictly speaking was a propylaeum, not an arch). 'It was big, black and beautiful,' he told me, 'and there was a melancholy about it, with all the people wandering through on their bland business.' Michael Palin is currently a patron of the Euston Arch Trust, but 'Dan Cruickshank' is the correct answer. Amid the construction site at Euston is a hoarding on which is written a 'Euston Timeline'. There is no mention of the Arch.

49. They all own (or owned) model railway layouts.

50. Elton John; the album was *Tumbleweed Connection*.

51. '9 to 5', about a woman whose days are apparently dormant until the man in her life comes home, which he does by train.

52. Painting pictures of railway scenes.

53. Willie Rushton, a regular player of the game 'Mornington Crescent', on the Radio 4 comedy *I'm Sorry I Haven't a Clue*. The French version, according to a history of the game written by the programme makers, is called Mornington Croissant.

54. Stiff Records. Among the performers on board were Lene Lovich, Micky Jupp, Jona Lewie and Rachel Sweet.

55. Prue Leith, who was the first woman appointed to the board. She set about overhauling the catering.

56. Kirsty Wark. 'Now my ritual usually consists of a quick catch-up with the staff in the lounge car as they put ice in my glass and I choose my malt of the night,' she wrote in *The New Statesman* in 2014.

57. Paul Atterbury, and a very nice man he is, too.

58. Request stops.

59. The Cornish comedian Jethro (Geoffrey McIntyre Rowe), who was known for his 'blue' material. 'This train don't stop Camborne Wednesdays' is on YouTube and, being one of Jethro's cleaner routines, is (almost) suitable for family viewing.

CRIMINALS AND CRIME

60. Pickpockets (strictly, 'Railway Pickpockets') – from *London Labour and the London Poor* (1862) by Henry Mayhew.

61. Hop-pickers.

62. He wrote crime stories set on railways, principally in *Thrilling Stories of the Railway* (1911). His detective is Thorpe Hazell, a healthy-eating faddist, keen on 'physical jerks'.

63. Charles Tyson Yerkes, who electrified the District Line and built the Bakerloo, Piccadilly and Charing Cross, Euston & Hampstead Railways. He also founded the Underground Electric Railways of London, the forerunner of London Transport. He had been imprisoned for fraud.

64. Reading Gaol, from the Great Western Main Line. It closed in 1914. At the time of writing its fate remains uncertain.

65. *The Mikado* (1885), by Gilbert and Sullivan. The Mikado was explaining how he would make the punishment fit the crime. As to the meaning of 'Parliamentary Train', see question 522.

66. Seven murders were committed in that time.

67. The identities of five of the killers are known:

1. On 9 July 1864 Franz Müller killed Thomas Briggs on the North London Railway.

2. On 27 June 1881 Percy Lefroy killed Isaac Gold on the London, Brighton & South Coast Railway.

3. On 12 February 1897, Elizabeth Camp was found dead of head wounds in a compartment on the arrival of a London & South Western train from Feltham at Waterloo. A chemist's pestle with blood and hair upon it was found by the side of the line, but the identity of the killer remains unknown.

4. On 17 January 1901 George Henry Parker murdered William Pearson on a train near Surbiton.

5. In 1905 another murder occurred on the LB&SCR, and whereas the previous victim had been called 'Gold' this one was called 'Money' – so it was as if the people were killed for the value of their names. The mutilated body of Mary Money was found in Merstham Tunnel on 24 September. She had probably been thrown from the train. Nobody was ever charged with the crime, but the likely killer was Robert 'Hicks' Murray, Miss Money's brother, who in 1912 would commit suicide after murdering six people – two sisters (to both of whom Murray was married) and four children – in Eastbourne.

6. On 18 March 1910, John Alexander Dickman killed John Nisbet on the East Coast Main Line between Newcastle and Alnmouth.

7. On 8 January 1914, Willie Starchfield, aged five, was found dead, apparently strangled, on a train at Haggerston Station in East London. His father was charged, but the judge stopped the case and instructed the jury to acquit.

68. Small apertures between compartments, introduced to reduce the isolation of compartment travellers after Franz Müller killed Thomas Briggs, as mentioned above. They are also (albeit with a capital 'L' on the second word) 'rich, creamy-tasting, fat-free' yoghurts.

69. *The Mystery of the Blue Train* (1928).

70. Any answer involving the phrase 'Brighton Trunk Murder' would be correct. There were two. On 17 June, a female torso was found inside a trunk at Brighton Station left luggage office. The legs were later found in the left luggage office at King's Cross. Neither the victim nor the killer was ever identified. The investigation of this first Brighton Trunk Murder unearthed a second one: the body of Violet Kaye was found in a trunk at 52 Kemp Street, a house recently vacated by one Henry Mancini, who was tried for murder but acquitted. On the strength of these crimes, Brighton's boast that it was 'the Queen of the Watering Places' was turned against it, and it became 'the Queen of the Slaughtering Places'.

71. c. Mr Dean had pleaded not guilty on the grounds that it was better to have pulled the communication cord than snatch the cigarette from the smoker's lips, which he felt a strong urge to do, and which would almost certainly have led to violence, and perhaps serious injury. He also said that the smell of cigarette smoke made him ill. The fine was two pounds.

72. Ernest 'Ernie' Marples, who had installed Dr Beeching as BR chairman, and whose firm built roads while he was promoting railway closures. He bolted on *The Night Ferry* in 1975, entraining in Paris for Monaco, where he died in 1978.

73. 'The Poacher Line'.

74. Layouts of the Market Deeping Model Railway Club were destroyed by three schoolboy vandals. 'Over 1,000 emails and messages of support have been received,' reported the club's website, adhering to the passive voice favoured by railway writers, 'along with financial donations from over 5,500 people from across the world'. These included £10,500 from Sir Rod Stewart, a railway modeller himself. (His massive layout shows industrial scenes in an imaginary city, based on 1940s Chicago and New York. Interviewed in the December 2019 issue of *Railway Modeller* magazine, Sir Rod said, 'I find beauty in what everyone else sees as ugly – rugged skyscrapers, beaten-up warehouses, things that are very run down.' He elaborated on *The Jeremy Vine Show* on BBC Radio 2: 'You start off with a grey. And then you add a little concrete colour so every paving stone is slightly different. And the cracks have to have some black chalk … and then you add a little bit of rubbish to the gutters.' While on tour he would book extra hotel rooms so that he could work on the model buildings. When the BBC News website covered the story of Sir Rod's layout in November 2019, the headline was 'I am railing'.)

The Market Deeping Model Railway Club has established a charitable trust with the money, one of whose aims is to 'disseminate through education projects the arts and skills involved in railway modelling'.

75. This is William Wordsworth protesting, in 'A Just Disdain' (1844), against the incursion of the railway into the Lake District.

76. Mrs Gamp, in *Martin Chuzzlewit* (1844).

77. Mr Weller (father of Sam Weller), in *Master Humphrey's Clock* (1840).

78. Wilkie Collins. In an article for the website of the Wilkie Collins Society, Erika Behrisch Elce wrote that Collins takes an 'immersive' approach 'at odds with the popular Cook tours and organised guidebooks from John Murray insinuating themselves along the newly opened passenger railways and beyond'.

79. Walter Bagehot (who is, after all, the *only* constitutional historian) in *The English Constitution* (1867). It's a neat argument against High Speed 2.

80. John Ruskin. He did not like railways and here, in a letter to *The Times* of 3 March 1887, his critique is distilled. Probably Ruskin's most famous utterance on railways concerned the building, in 1863, by the Midland Railway of a viaduct traversing the river Wye in Monsal Vale in Derbyshire. The utterance was couched in a supposed letter of 1871, addressed to 'the Workmen and Labourers of Great Britain': 'The valley

is gone, and the Gods with it; and now, every fool in Buxton can be at Bakewell in half-an-hour, and every fool in Bakewell in Buxton'. Today, the *railway* is gone, but the viaduct survives and is Grade Two listed.

In *Proust*, a biography of Marcel Proust, Edmund White wrote, 'Ruskin was appalled by the effects of unbridled capitalism on the proletariat. Against the horrors of the machine age, Ruskin championed a utopian vision of the independent artisan … It is difficult for people today to understand the enormous influence Ruskin (1819–1900) exerted everywhere in the last decades of the nineteenth century.'

81. *Three Men in a Boat* by Jerome K. Jerome (1889).

82. Waterloo.

83. The Russian Revolution. In *The Official British Rail Book of Trains for Young People*, Michael Bowler wrote that, in light of the Russian Revolution, 'any form of socialism smacked of Bolshevism and was not to be tolerated'. It might be said that, 130 years earlier, the French Revolution had created a similar mood against state power, so ensuring that Britain's railways would be allowed to develop in private hands.

84. *Railway Ribaldry*.

85. *Oh, Dr Beeching!* It ran for two series, between 1995 and 1997.

86. *Private Eye*.

87. David Hare.

ENTHUSIASTS

88. Thomas Arnold, enlightened headmaster of Rugby School from 1828 to 1841.

89. George Augustus Nokes (which is Sekon backwards).

90. In 2007. I was a member from 2004, and I knew the club was not long for this world. In my early forties, I was the youngest member by about twenty years, and their annual dinners began with a toast to the Queen.

91. The Model Railway Club, which is entitled to that very elemental title by being (according to *The Guinness Book of Records*) the very first model railway club, having been founded in 1910. The club's most famous layout is Copenhagen Fields, which depicts in 2 mm scale the railway approach to King's Cross and surrounding streets roughly as they would have looked in 1955, when the King's Cross-set film *The Ladykillers* was released. The club likes to describe King's Cross at the time as 'a site of outstanding unnatural beauty'. The model is collapsible, and is sometimes taken on tour, since 'the whole ensemble fits into a 35cwt Luton headed Transit van'.

92. Railway modelling, and the book was *The Craft of Modelling Railways*.

93. C. Hamilton Ellis; it was published in 1947.

94. Nock, Rolt, Allen. Railway writers do tend to like initials in
their bylines. *Railways, A Readers' Guide*, by E. T. Bryant, is
a veritable alphabet soup of initials. He cites, among many
others, J. I. C. Boyd, M. J. T. Lewis, N. R. P. Bonsor, J. C. and
F. Inglis, F. A. S. Brown, F. G. B. Atkinson and, best of all,
R. O. T. Povey, who wrote a history of the Keighley & Worth
Valley Railway.

95. Aircraft spotters of the Second World War. The term was
applied to rail enthusiasts from 1945, when Ian Allan formed
the 'Spotters' Club'.

96. The Railway Correspondence & Travel Society, formed in
1928. In *The Railway Dictionary*, Alan A. Jackson writes that it
is 'one of the largest British organisations for rly enthusiasts,
primarily catering to those obsessed by the fine detail of
day-to-day operations, particularly by the locos, trains
and rolling stock, their movements and their numbering'.
Jackson adds that it is 'affectionately known as "the Royal
Corps of Train Spotters"'.

97. Gricer. The term became popular in the 1970s. An undergricer
– or Undergricer – favours the London Underground.

98. An enthusiast's specialism, the aim being to cover the full
extent of every possible stretch of track, especially sections
not normally accessible to the public.

99. The first sight of a certain engine. Usually the number will
be taken.

100. b. Howling!

101. To trespass in a locomotive depot in order to 'cop' locos.

102. Mark Smith is the Man in Seat 61. He created the railway travel information website www.seat61.com, which is named after his favourite Eurostar seat. 'Zaharoff, the notorious arms dealer, would always book compartment 7 on the Orient Express to or from Istanbul,' explains Smith, formerly the manager of Charing Cross Station. 'On Eurostar, I would always request seat 61 … as it lines up with the window, one of a cosy pair of seats facing each other across a table complete with table lamp, like an old Pullman car.'

103. TWERPS.

104. *Platform Souls*, and it's the best book about trainspotting.

105. Transport 2000.

106. Michael Palin.

107. Christian Wolmar.

STAFF

108. A meal eaten on duty.

109. Firing – that is, putting coal on the fire.

110. Returning from a shift by travelling as a normal passenger.

111. Guard.

112. To quote from *Inside Underground Railways* by Alan A. Jackson, 'to filter the smoke a bit before they breathed it'. The Metropolitan Railway, opened in 1863, was an idea ahead of its time, in that subterraneum railways really require electric traction. The drivers and firemen had to seek special permission from the management to grow their beards.

113. Excessive use of the whistle.

114. *Through the Looking Glass, and What Alice Found There* (1871), by Lewis Carroll.

115. The Great Eastern Railway.

116. These supposed flowers or plants are all the names of station masters. (And they're all station masters on the Midland Railway, but that qualification is not required for a correct answer.)

117. The poem is called 'To A Great Western Broad-Gauge Engine and Its Stoker'. The last broad-gauge service left Paddington at 10.15 a.m. on 20 May 1892. Within three days the last 213 miles of broad-gauge track were taken up.

118. A buttonhole flower.

119. York Station, showing its staff. The image was used on a postcard. In some versions of this picture, the sign reading 'Gentlemen's Lavatory' has been excised.

120. 1907.

121. They held national strikes – in the latter year as part of the General Strike.

122. They didn't have to wear a uniform.

123. Crewe, the home of the LNWR's vast works, and the site of six important railway junctions.

124. Gertrude Bell, the writer and traveller.

125. He asks Toad to 'wash a few shirts for me', Toad being disguised (obviously successfully) as a washerwoman.

126. To test the soundness of carriage or carriage wheels. A brief clang signified a healthy wheel. If a crack had formed, the wheel made a hollow, ringing sound.

127. His portable lunch, dinner or indeed breakfast. From the snap fastening of a metal lunchbox.

128. He or she checked tickets at the barrier.

129. A fireman, his shovel being the banjo.

130. Overtime.

131. Manchester United. The club began life as the Newton Heath Lancashire & Yorkshire Railway Football Club. The name was changed to Manchester United in 1902.

132. Public Relations Consultant. (John Elliot later said that he never knew whether, having brought PR to the UK, he should have been commemorated by a statue in Parliament Square or 'publicly hanged on Waterloo Bridge'.)

133. Frank Pick. As vice-chairman of London Underground between 1933 and 1940, he was in effect the head of design. He had been in a similar role at LT's predecessor, the Underground Group. We have Pick to thank for the Underground roundel, the Johnston typeface, the Underground map, the railway stations of Charles Holden, and many other aesthetic phenomena.

134. Harry Beck. He was paid about five guineas for it.

135. He always wore his hat backwards, as if he wanted to streamline *himself*. When *Mallard* passed 113 mph, it had broken the British steam speed record, set by another Gresley engine, *Silver Fox*, but then Duddington decided to beat the *world* steam record, which had been set by the Germans at 124.5 mph. 'Duddington pushed Mallard still harder,' writes Don Hale in *Mallard: How the Blue Streak Broke the World Speed Record*, 'perhaps lengthening the cut-off as far as he could to get every last breath of steam from the boiler into her three voracious cylinders ...'

136. a. 690,000.

137. a. 190,000.

138. b. About 53,000.

139. Railmen.

140. In 1948, when British Railways took over.

141. Mills was hit with an iron bar during the Great Train Robbery of 1963; he never fully recovered from his injuries.

142. c. The regulator: this is the lever that admits the steam to the cylinders and so makes the engine go. It is the equivalent of the accelerator. The one in the photograph is on an engine belonging to the Bodmin & Wenford preserved railway in Cornwall, which offers steam engine driving courses that are very well taught – with delicious and authentic Cornish pasties for lunch. Students are advised that, for all its primitive appearance, the regulator is highly sensitive. You only need to move it an inch to set the engine rolling.

143. Dr Beeching (BR chairman 1961–65). Beeching – who was not a medical doctor – is said to have 'chain-smoked' cigars. He preferred payment in kind, maintaining that the tax on any monetary fee was so high as to make the fee not worth having.

144. c. Four. They were: Olive Clarke OBE, JP, chairman of the Transport Users' Consultative Committee for the North West; Gladys Fowke, Management Services Manager of Thos. T. Ward (Railway Engineers); Jose M. Johnson, MBE, Secretary of the Railway Division of the Institute of Mechanical Engineers; Mrs Alison Munro CBE, Chairman, Central Transport Consultative Committee.

145. Bob Reid – *Sir* Bob Reid, indeed. In full, their names were Sir Robert Basil Reid (1983–90) and Sir Robert Paul Reid (1990–95).

146. An electric multiple unit or a railcar.

147. 'The wrong type of snow.'

148. *In loco parentis*.

CHILDREN

149. Isambard Kingdom Brunel. The coin became lodged in his windpipe. His father, Marc, suggested he be strapped to a board and turned upside down, and by this means it was jerked loose.

150. Roberta (or Bobbie) was the eldest, then came Peter, then Phyllis.

151. Roberta was played by Jenny Agutter, Peter by Gary Warren, and Phyllis by Sally Thomsett, who played the youngest character in spite of being the oldest of the three actors. In the film, she was playing a 'little girl' while nearly twenty, and her contract precluded her from being seen near the set driving, smoking or in the company of her boyfriend.

152. Gamage's. The shop in Holborn featured a large model railway with day and night scenes created by lighting effects.

153. c. Twenty-one. The editor was H. Golding.

154. The railway writer, Cecil J. Allen, when writing for children. There was also 'Uncle Mac' (A. B. MacLeod).

155. 'Among the victims were two young children'. Rolt continues.

> Their charred bodies were unrecognisable and their
> identity was never established. It seems unbelievable that
> two children should board a long-distance express without
> someone, parent, relative or guardian, being aware of
> the fact, or missing them if they were playing truant. Yet
> nobody came forward to claim them, nor could they be
> connected with any of the other victims of the accident.
> They were buried in an unnamed grave in Charfield
> churchyard.

Locals reported that between 1929 and the late 1950s a woman
dressed in black made frequent visits to the memorial to
the crash victims inside the church. Any answer involving
'unidentified child victims' would be correct.

156. Railway arches. Tupper was a middle-distance runner who
appeared in the *Rover* comic from 1949, then *Victor* until 1992.
He was a working-class man, and a perennial underdog,
fated to compete against privileged *Chariots of Fire* types. He
had various humble jobs but worked mainly as a welder in
a workshop under a railway arch; for a period he also lived
under the arch.

157. Keith Chegwin. Any child who joined received 'five pounds
worth of travel vouchers, twenty sticker station stamps to
give discounted entry to places of interest around the country,
membership card, giant 3.36m (11ft) full-colour poster and *Rail
Riders Express*, a full-colour, fun-packed magazine, packed with
features about railways, competitions, and a free gift with
every issue'. They were also entitled to free entry to the Rail
Riders World Model Railway at York Station.

158. Those featuring the *Wombles*.

159. The title denoted a locomotive, but locomotive names are not usually prefaced with the definite article (whereas train names *are*); accordingly, the title of the second series was changed to *Flockton Flyer*. The programme was filmed on the West Somerset Railway.

160. c. Five.

161. *Ivor the Engine.*

162. GWR. The aim, according to the ad agency involved, is to get passengers to revalue rail 'by bringing to life the adventure and excitement that its customers can access while using much-loved characters to build appreciation and loyalty'.

POLITICIANS

163. Addington. That is, Henry Addington, 1st Viscount Sidmouth. He was preceded and succeeded as prime minister by William Pitt the Younger, who was considered the more charismatic and effective operator.

164. William Ewart Gladstone. As President of the Board of Trade, he introduced, in 1844, the Regulation of Railways Act, one of whose provisions gave Parliament the power to nationalise any railway company making a profit of more than 10 per cent.

165. The Metropolitan Railway of 1863.

166. John Stuart Mill.

167. Arthur Balfour, who was prime minister between 1902 and 1905. His father was James Maitland Balfour.

168. Stanley Baldwin, who also hated cars. On the other hand, he was a director of the Great Western Railway (of which his father had been chairman).

169. Frank Hornby, who invented Meccano, Hornby Trains and Dinky Toys. 'Meccano' incidently, is thought to be a corruption of the phrase 'make and know'.

170. Barbara Castle. She developed the idea of the 'social railway' (the utility of even uneconomic lines), which undermined Dr Beeching's purely economic rationale for railway closures, albeit not until most of his closure programme was complete.

171. William 'Willie' Whitelaw, whose railwayman grandfather – also called William Whitelaw – was chairman of the LNER from 1923 to 1938.

172. Bob Cryer.

173. Ann Cryer, who was married to Bob Cryer.

174. Jimmy Knapp, a Scottish ex-signalman. In 1990 the NUR merged with the National Union of Seamen to form the National Union of Rail, Maritime and Transport Workers (RMT).

175. False. Between 1988 and 1990 he was Minister of State for Transport, in other words a junior minister. During his time in the post he is credited with having saved the Settle & Carlisle Railway from closure, so acquiring the railway credibility that underpins his role as a presenter of railway TV programmes. At the time of writing he is President of the Friends of the Settle & Carlisle Line.

ANIMALS

176. Slough Station, Platform 5, but 'Slough Station' will do. The dog is (or was) Station Jim, the most famous of the 'dog collectors'. A dog collector loped around the platforms of a station with a leather box on its back, into which passengers were invited to donate to charity. Station Jim collected at Slough Station for the Great Western Railway Widows and Orphans Fund between 1894 and 1896. Apparently, he would bark a thank you for every deposited coin. In *Lambert's Railway Miscellany*, Anthony Lambert identifies several other dog collectors, including Brum II, who collected at Euston for the London & North Western Railway Servants' Benevolent Fund between 1910 and 1917, and Laddie, who collected at Waterloo. He is now at the National Railway Museum in York, having been stuffed, like Station Jim.

177. Packs of hounds.

178. The St Leger horse race meeting. In *What the Railways Did for Us*, Stuart Hylton writes that the coming of the railway to Doncaster transformed the St Leger 'into a major entertainment for working people'.

179. Skimbleshanks, from Eliot's *Old Possum's Book of Practical Cats* and the musical *Cats*, which was based on Eliot's book.

180. Racing pigeons. They would travel on 'pigeon specials' (trains loaded with pigeon baskets) and then release the birds at the designated starting point of the race.

181. a. 9,000.

182. a. Charlie. He had worked at Newmarket, principally engaged – fittingly enough – in shunting horseboxes.

183. A giraffe. Tri-ang Hornby, a very imaginative company, also produced an 'Exploding Car': 'Hit this lethally laden freight car with a missile from either of the Tri-Ang Railways Rocket Launchers and it will explode most realistically.'

184. 'School excursions to Bristol Zoo.' But unadorned 'zoo excursion' is acceptable.

185. In the ladies' lavatory at Paddington Station, but 'Paddington Station' will do. In *Lambert's Railway Miscellany*, Anthony Lambert writes that Tiddles

> was adopted in 1970 as a six-week-old kitten by the ladies' lavatory attendant June Watson. She took him home one day, thinking he would like a conventional domain, but Tiddles much preferred to snooze in the corner of the station lavatory. The reason became all too apparent as the fat cat enjoyed a high-fat, high-calorie diet of chicken livers, kidneys, rabbit and steak brought in by admirers and kept in his personal fridge.

Tiddles died, weighing 32 lbs, in 1983.

186. Two. They must both be on a lead or in a basket, and they must not occupy a seat, or a charge will be made.

187. The Tarka Line (aka the North Devon Line) was named after Tarka the otter, eponymous hero of Williamson's novel.

188. *The Wrong Trousers*, starring Wallace and Gromit. 'Nods to silent movies' train chases', writes Ian Carter, with strong approval, in his book *Railways and Culture in Britain*.

189. c. 1,000 tons, according to Benedict le Vay in his excellent book *Britain from the Rails*.

190. A duck, specifically a mallard. Gresley was fond of wildfowl, in the sense that he was fond of shooting them, hence his naming his most famous engine *Mallard*. In the original design for the statue, he was pictured standing next to a mallard, but his grandchildren felt this was 'demeaning', so the mallard was removed.

TOPOGRAPHY

THE PERMANENT WAY

(RAILWAY TRACK AND ASSOCIATED FEATURES)

191. Ballast. 'The term "ballast" in connection with railway track originated on Tyneside,' writes John Marshall in *The Guinness Railway Book*. 'The ships which carried coal from Newcastle returned "in ballast", laden with gravel and other material to maintain stability. This ballast was dumped by the quays and was used to provide a solid base for the tramways which carried the coal. The name "ballast" was continued on the tramways and became a standard railway term.'

192. The distance between the running rails.

193. Seven foot and one quarter-inch.

194. Narrow gauge.

195. False: it's 1 foot 11½ inches.

196. a. 2,112.

197. Six thousand miles.

198. Trains (in general) run on the left.

199. The movement of a signal arm, in *The Lazy Tour of Two Idle Apprentices* (1857). Or the author might have been Wilkie Collins, since they wrote the book together, but it seems like a Dickensian image.

200. Lineside telegraph wires.

201. They are the 'cut-and-cover', 'sub-surface' or (more vividly) the 'shallow' lines, and any of those would be right. These lines, comprising about 40 per cent of the London Underground, were built just below the surface, usually by making a road into a trench, inserting the railway, then roofing over the trench (so recreating the road) with girders. The 'Tubes', which are deeper, came later.

202. The negative conductor rail.

203. Compressing the ballast under the sleepers, usually with a machine.

204. Of lines serving London, 'Up' is towards London, 'Down' is away from it. The terms can't apply *in* London, hence 'Eastbound', 'Westbound', 'Northbound', 'Southbound' on the London Underground.

205. His brother, Mycroft. Holmes said it in 'The Adventure of the Bruce-Partington Plans'.

206. A marshalling yard, of which there are none left. They resembled multiple sidings, where goods trains were assembled, often at night, from numerous and diverse wagons. In *Yesterday's Trains*, Peter Herring wrote of marshalling yards, 'Off-key clanging, like the peal of cracked church bells, stood for the city at night.' That enemy of romance Dr Beeching killed them off with his rationalisation of freight, whereby 'wagon-load' would be replaced by 'train-load': diverse trains of various goods were replaced by uniform trains of (usually sealed) wagons all containing the same thing.

207. An artificial mound created in a marshalling yard, from which a wagon could move by gravity to the right siding.

208. In upper-quadrant signalling, a horizontal signal means stop, and a driver can proceed if the arm is raised through about forty-five degrees; in lower-quadrant, a horizontal arm also means stop and the driver can proceed if the arm is *lowered*. Upper-quadrant would seem more logical, because a 'proceed' signal, having to work against gravity, would be less likely to arise by accident. But the GWR always liked to be different.

209. Stoke Bank.

210. On the Settle & Carlisle Line in Yorkshire, between Ribblehead and Dent. It's 1-in-100 for 15 miles.

211. The Shap incline, between Oxenholme and Penrith on the West Coast Main Line.

212. 'Beattock', which is short for Beattock Bank. It starts 50 miles north of Carlisle and lasts 10 miles. The gradient is between 1-in-88 and 1-in-74.

213. At Dawlish in Devon where, but for the Wall, the train would be on the beach. The term is also sometimes used to denote the whole stretch from Exeter to Newton Abbot. Either answer will do.

214. a. A third: about 6,000 of the 18,000 miles, and most of its recommendations were carried out.

215. The summit station of the Snowdon Mountain Railway, 3,540 feet above sea level.

216. London Underground. The Dollis Brook Viaduct, over Dollis Road (and the Dollis Brook), carries trains between Finchley Central and Mill Hill East on the Northern Line.

217. Whistle. In *Britain from the Rails*, Benedict le Vay notes that the signs are anachronistic because, while steam engines had whistles, modern trains have horns. 'If you see a "W", probably to your left,' he continues, 'or hear a hoot, keep an eye out a quarter-mile further for what it might be protecting – possibly a crossing or a footpath.'

218. Margaret Thatcher, who didn't *often* go by rail. According to Andrew Murray in *Off the Rails* (about railway privatisation), she travelled by train 'only once in the eleven years of her premiership'. Murray's book, incidentally, begins, 'It didn't even seem like a good idea at the time.'

219. Subsidy.

PARTICULAR RAILWAY LINES AND COMPANIES

220. Leeds. It was the first railway to use steam successfully, from 1812 (although it reverted to being horse-drawn in 1835). Today, part of the line is operated as a preserved railway.

221. The Stockton & Darlington Railway. Shildon is known as 'the first railway town'.

222. The Liverpool–Manchester was the first inter-city railway, the first to use only steam, the first to be fully timetabled and signalled, the first to be entirely double-tracked and the first to carry mail.

223. It was London's first railway. To save money on land acquisition it ran entirely on a viaduct, which had 878 arches. Businesses then occupied those arches.

224. It announced that it would be running Sunday excursions.

225. It is said, by some, to be the first railway to close.

226. The builder and operator of the last main line into London was the Great Central Railway. Grand Central Rail (no definite article) is the name of a present-day open-access train operator running services mainly on the East Coast Main Line.

227. Fictional. It's the railway in *The Railway Children*. There once was a Great Eastern & Western Railway, though.

228. You can use either; this is one of the few routes over which competition between railway companies has been possible.

229. b. Melton Constable.

230. Although it was a standard-gauge railway, it was not connected to the national network, being cut off from it by the river Torridge. The BWH!AR is also the only railway company name in the UK to incorporate an exclamation mark. The mark comes from Charles Kingsley's novel of 1855, *Westward Ho!*, which was set in nearby Bideford. When a holiday settlement was created near Bideford, it was named after Kingsley's novel.

231. The Withered Arm was the route – more formally called the North Cornwall Line – created by the London & South Western Railway running west of Exeter, through North Devon and into Cornwall. It was closed by Beeching, leaving Devon and Cornwall served only by the more southerly route forged by the Great Western. The line was beautiful, but economically marginal, hence its great romantic appeal. It was named 'the Withered Arm' by the railway author T. W. E. Roche at the time of its closure.

232. The London & North Western Railway, the justification being that it incorporated the route of the pioneering Liverpool & Manchester Railway.

233. The Bakerloo – because it connected (before being extended) Waterloo and Baker Street. The official name was originally the Baker Street & Waterloo Railway, but Nichols's tag was formally adopted in 1906, much to the disgust of the *Railway Magazine*: 'for a railway itself to adopt its gutter title, is not what we expect from a railway company.'

234. c. The Midland: comfortable trains (even in Third Class), and the most scenic – if not the most direct – route to Scotland via the Settle & Carlisle Line and the Waverley Route to Edinburgh.

235. Colonel Holman Fred Stephens. The lines were part of his empire of scruffy and makeshift light railways, which he either built or managed, always with economy uppermost in mind. Stephens, who was the son of the art critic and pre-Raphaelite Frederick George Stephens, ran his dozen or so railways from 23 Salford Terrace, Tonbridge, Kent.

236. The LMS; it ran into England, Wales and Scotland.

237. The Southern. Its territory – squeezed between London and the South Coast – was too small to require them. But in the *Dad's Army* episode, 'The Royal Train', it is implied that the Southern did have water troughs. Since Mainwaring's men are notionally based on the South Coast, yet they are splashed by a passing locomotive collecting water when they await the King at their local station, Walmington-on-Sea. (This episode was filmed at Weybourne Station on the North Norfolk Railway.)

238. The Liverpool Overhead Railway, which opened in 1893, and ran along the Liverpool Docks. One of its stations, Dingle (the terminus), was actually underground. The last train ran on the night of 30 December 1956. 'Sirens from ships all along the waterfront wailed a tribute through the cold night air,' writes Michael Williams in *The Trains Now Departed*. 'At one station staff wept as they passed the station cat through a train window to a passenger who had offered to adopt it.'

239. A jigsaw. The GWR produced more jigsaws than any other of the Big Four: about eighty, as against the LNER's three. Other GWR titles included 'Cornish Riviera Express', 'Sir Francis Drake at Plymouth', 'Swansea Docks', 'Ann Hathaway's Cottage'.

240. The Talyllyn Railway is usually taken to be the first preserved railway. This narrow-gauge slate line first opened in 1865 and nearly closed in 1951, but was saved by some historically-minded rail enthusiasts – in particular by the author L. T. C. Rolt, who wrote a book about the episode, *Railway Adventure*, which is now regarded as a classic.

241. The Ffestiniog Railway. This is Bessie Jones, station master at Tan-y-Bwlch Station between 1929 and 1965. She greeted the trains in Welsh national costume.

242. The North Yorkshire Moors Railway.

243. Aviemore.

244. The Ffestiniog, the Welsh Highland, and (the hard one, because it's small) the Welsh Highland Heritage Railway.

245. The BR 'double arrow' logo, which pointed both ways.

246. *A Hard Day's Night.* What became the West Somerset Railway was, at the time, the Minehead Branch of BR Western Region. Scenes were also shot at Marylebone.

247. The Great Eastern Hotel at Liverpool Street and the Great Northern at King's Cross. The Great Eastern Hotel is now called Andaz London Liverpool Street.

248. So as to preserve the initials 'N. B.', by which the Hotel was familiarly known. Today, the 'New' has been dropped. Of course, they could just have kept the original name.

249. False. Britain had a maglev railway between Birmingham International Airport and Birmingham International Station, from 1984 to 1995. Its advanced technology notwithstanding, it was a low-speed shuttle.

250. The North London Line (originally Richmond to North Woolwich) – known for late and cancelled trains, and frightening, under-staffed railway stations. It is now part of London Overground. The North London Line had its origins in the North London Railway, which in turn grew out of the inelegantly named East & West India Docks & Birmingham Junction Railway.

251. False, although people could be forgiven for thinking otherwise. The Elizabeth Line is operated by MTR Elizabeth Line, the private business that operates the concession, not by TfL, which runs the Undergound. It is, however, part of the 'TfL Network'; it is also on the Tube Map, albeit with a double line (like the Overground) rather than the solid line of a Tube line. The suffix 'Line' suggests it *is* a Tube line, but the fact that the word 'Line' is included in its labelling on the Tube Map suggests it is not.

STATIONS

252. A halt.

253. True; and it is the opening assertion of *London's Great Railway Stations*, by Oliver Green.

254. A whirlwind.

255. 1837: Euston.
1838: Paddington.
1852: King's Cross.

256. Waterloo, with twenty-four.

257. Paddington. The 'lawn' used to be the circulating area at the head of the platforms; it is now more like a shopping centre. It is so called because it used to be the station master's garden. Apparently, a young boy was once prosecuted for picking a flower from it.

258. Fenchurch Street.

259. Euston, in 1848.

260. King's Cross, by Lewis Cubitt.

261. Liverpool Street, which opened in 1864, is named after nearby Liverpool Street, which was named in 1827 after the longest serving prime minister of the nineteenth century, Lord Liverpool (Robert Banks Jenkinson). But 'The station is named after Lord Liverpool' will do as an answer.

262. Camille Pissarro. He was living in Upper Norwood at the time.

263. No. It was closed in 1954.

264. Baker Street and Gower Street, which in 1909 was renamed Euston Square.

265. St Enoch. It was closed by Beeching and demolished in 1977. In *The Trains Now Departed*, Michael Williams writes that 'St Enoch had many fine features, including a special room for travelling salesmen to show off their samples – the only one in Britain.'

266. An island platform.

267. Two were required from the following:

Cheltenham Spa St James Station (now closed).
St James Park Station, in Exeter.
Paisley St James Station.
St James Street Station, on London Overground.
Liverpool St James Station (now closed).
St James's Park Station, on the London Underground.
St James Metro station, on the Tyne & Wear Metro.

268. On the concourse of Blackfriars Station, London. These panels were on the façade of the original station, opened in 1886 by the London, Chatham & Dover Railway, and they boast of the range of destinations available from the station, including the exotic (e.g. Turin – 'available' only in the sense that you could get there eventually from Blackfriars, if you changed trains many times) and the less exotic (e.g. Bromley). The panels were put inside the station during a rebuild in the 1970s. Blackfriars was rebuilt again more recently.

269. They all have, or have had, stations with the suffix 'Victoria'.

270. Three. They are Pontefract Baghill, Pontefract Monkhill, Pontefract Tanshelf.

271. Marylebone, in his book, *London's Historic Railway Stations*. 'As quiet as Marylebone on the Sabbath' used to be a saying.

272. Paddington. See 'The Adventure of the Engineer's Thumb', in which he remarks that 'railway cases are seldom trivial'.

273. Because it was a fire risk.

274. Thurso.

275. The living and the dead. The façade is that of the railway station formerly belonging to the London Necropolis & Mausoleum Company, which carried corpses and mourners by rail to Brookwood Cemetery in Surrey. The station, which opened in 1902, replaced the first one of the Necropolis Company, which had opened a few hundred yards away in 1854 but was demolished to allow the expansion of Waterloo Station. The Necropolis Company ceased operations after its platforms were damaged in an air raid of 1941, but the business

had been in decline for decades. Today the building is owned by a shipping company.

276. Arsenal. Gillespie Road station was opened on the Great Northern, Piccadilly & Brompton Railway in 1906. It was renamed Arsenal in 1932, after the football club, which had been playing at nearby Highbury Stadium since 1913. Arsenal FC had originally played in Woolwich, being the football team of the arsenal there (Woolwich being the base of the Royal Artillery), hence the name.

277. In *The Railway Station: A Social History*, Jeffrey Richards and John M. Mackenzie name the hallmarks of a Jennings convenience: 'penny in the slot, flushing lavatories, wash-out urinals'.

278. Glasgow Central Station. The picture shows 'the Shell', a Howitzer shell that had been turned into a charity collecting box after the First World War. It stood in the middle of the concourse until 1966 (it is now near one of the exits). An arrangement to meet 'by the Shell' was the Glasgow Central equivalent of 'under the clock' at Waterloo or Victoria.

279. That confusing place, London Bridge. It is the start of a poem called 'London Bridge', by the unjustly forgotten John Davidson (1858–1909). He wrote an equally good poem about Liverpool Street, which begins:

> Through crystal roofs the sunlight fell,
> And pencilled beams the gloss renewed
> On iron rafters balanced well
> On iron struts; though dimly hued,
> With smoke o'erlaid, with dust endued,
> The walls and beams like beryl shone ...

280. c. Seven.

281. The companies were:

> The London & North Western Railway.
> The Caledonian Railway.
> The Midland Railway.
> The North British Railway.
> The Glasgow & South Western Railway.
> The Maryport & Carlisle Railway.
> The North Eastern Railway.

282. Wemyss Bay, of 1903, by James Miller, 'the dominant personality of Scottish railway architecture'.

283. Charing Cross. Six people died.

284. The judging of a Best-Kept Station Garden competition.

285. Arnos Grove, designed by Charles Holden, and opened on the Piccadilly Line in 1932.

286. They both had cinemas, showing news and cartoons. The novelist Andrew Barrow was (briefly, until he was sacked) assistant manager at the Waterloo one in 1966. In his amusing autobiographical novel *The Man in the Moon* he recalls:

> I wandered into the small auditorium and watched a newsreel about the Queen's visit to a football match, then a trailer featuring Alfred Hitchcock.
> 'I welcome you all here and feel sure we shall see some fine football,' said the Queen.
> 'How do you do?' said Alfred Hitchcock. 'I would like to tell you about my latest motion picture, *Marnie*.'

287. Surbiton. The style might be described as 'moderne' or 'Odeon Cinema style'.

288. King's Cross, Liverpool Street, Marylebone, Fenchurch Street. Strange, perhaps, that two of the smaller termini were included, but the selection of places for the Monopoly board was apparently made during a rather haphazard tour of London conducted by Victor Watson, MD of Leeds-based Waddington's (who manufactured the British version of the game), and his secretary Marjory Phillips in 1935. The two of them, for instance, included the Angel, Islington, which is not a street, but had once been a pub. It is thought that Watson and Phillips included it on the board to mark the fact that they'd taken refreshment during their tour in the Lyons tea room that stood on the site of the pub.

289. The Cannon Street Hotel, which fronted Cannon Street Station (and 'Cannon Street Station Hotel' will do as an answer). The hotel, along with most of the original station, was demolished between 1958 and 1960.

290. They are the numbers of people sheltering nightly from bombs in Underground stations. The first figure coincides with the Blitz; the second and third with the V1 and V2 rocket attacks.

291. Down Street. Winston Churchill would sometimes join them. It is said that the fumes from his dinners, plus the brandy fumes and cigar smoke, would drift along the tunnels, tormenting ordinary Londoners having to make do with jam sandwiches and tea served from watering cans as they sheltered in other stations along the line.

292. Milford Junction, supposedly in the Home Counties. (But in fact Carnforth, in Lancashire.)

293. They don't have entrance halls at ground level or any kind of surface building. This is a relatively rare occurrence on the Underground, whereas it is rare for stations on the Paris Metro to *have* them, because the city authorities felt they would spoil with the beauty of Paris.

294. A totem.

295. It was Titfield in *The Titfield Thunderbolt*.

296. Waterloo.

297. BRUTE stands for British Railways Universal Trolley Equipment. This denotes a small tractor that hauled open-topped wire net trucks. BRUTES carried parcels or luggage and were seen between 1964 and 1995.

298. Richmond Station Hotel, which incorporated the Crawdaddy Club, where the Rolling Stones had a residency until they got too big for the place. Today it is a restaurant. The nearby station is served by the national network, the District Line of the Underground, and London Overground.

299. Widnes – and Widnes is proud of the 'fact', even though the thrust of Simon's lyric is that he'd rather have been elsewhere. A plaque in the station ticket hall reads, 'It was while waiting at this station that Paul Simon was inspired to write the song "Homeward Bound".' It is the third plaque to that effect; the previous two were stolen. It is known that Simon was in Widnes in 1965 while waiting for a train to London, but there were two stations in the town at the time, and either one might have been the true location: there was Widnes North (which is what the one with the plaque was called until 1968) and Ditton, which closed in 1994, and which is perhaps the favourite since it had a direct connection to London, whereas from Widnes North you had to change. However, simple 'Widnes' will not do as an answer.

300. Paddington. The central character takes up residence there.

301. The Manchester Central Convention Complex. Better known as G-MEX.

302. Redbridge.

303. Because it's relatively little used.

304. St Pancras.

305. New Holland Pier Station was the terminus of a railway line and of the Humber Ferry which plied between New Holland Pier and Hull Corporation Pier. The ferry ceased operation – and the station was closed – in 1981 when the Humber Bridge was opened. There was no railway connection to Hull Corporation Pier, hence the possible (if tenuous) quiz question: 'Which BR station never saw any trains?' But you'd have to put 'station' in inverted commas. In *Goodbye to Yorkshire*, Roy Hattersley wrote of the ferry that it 'approached Hull in a great arc, half steaming, half drifting with the tide. It was squat, dirty and inhospitable. But despite all that, I passed some of my happiest moments standing on its deck or edging my way between the tethered motor cars to its lower saloon and bars.'

306. A piece of decorative board work on the edge of a
platform canopy.

307. a. Bradford.
b. Wakefield.

308. *Victoria Station*. It features a mini-cab controller trying to
persuade one of his drivers to go to Victoria Station.

309. Broad Street: *Give My Regards to Broad Street* (1984). Broad
Street Station in London was closed and demolished two years
later, although the roof had fallen in some years before.

310. One was in Birmingham, the forerunner of the present
Birmingham Snow Hill. It was opened by the Great Western
in 1912 and closed in 1972, then demolished – 'a short-sighted
act typical of its time', writes Paul Atterbury in *Tickets, Please:
A Nostalgic Journey Through Station Life*. It is now the Snow Hill
Car Park. The other was opened by the London, Chatham &
Dover Railway in 1974. It was near Holborn Viaduct, and in
1912 was renamed Holborn Viaduct Low Level.

311. Charing Cross.

312. Paddington. Their signature tune is 'Plymouth Ho'.

313. St John's Wood.

314. Vauxhall.

315. The Grade One-listed stations are:

> Birmingham Curzon Street (although it was closed as a
> station in 1966).
> Bristol Temple Meads.
> Huddersfield.
> King's Cross.
> Paddington.
> Manchester Liverpool Road.
> Newcastle.
> St James's Park (on the London Underground).
> St Pancras.

316. Birmingham New Street.

317. Uxbridge, on the Metropolitan Line. The machines contain no
cigarettes and (probably) would not work even if they did.

318. Fenchurch Street.

319. Norwich. The Wherry Lines go to Great Yarmouth and
Lowestoft; the Bittern Line to Sheringham; the Breckland
to Cambridge.

320. Truro; Penzance is the second busiest.

321. Cannon Street. The garden is actually on the roof of an
office building, which was built on the roof of the station in
the 1980s.

322. Birmingham New Street.

TUNNELS

323. Here is Alan A. Jackson in *The Railway Dictionary*: 'A railway tunnel is defined by BR civil engineers as any structure that carries the railway through or under a *natural* construction. Anything else is a "bridge", or "covered way".'

324. Ninety per cent.

325. No. The first railway tunnel in Britain, and indeed the world, is usually said to be Fritchley Tunnel, built in 1793 to accommodate the Butterley Gangroad, a horse-drawn railway connecting limestone quarries in Derbyshire with the Cromford Canal. The tunnel was later adapted for use by steam trains. The railway running through the tunnel fell into disuse from 1933, and the tunnel was sealed up in 1977.

326. Kilsby Tunnel on the West Coast Main Line, built by Robert Stephenson and opened in 1838, when it was the longest railway tunnel in the world. The photograph shows one of two ventilation shafts, built to reassure passengers that they would not suffocate.

327. The sun is said to shine right through the tunnel on the occasion of the birthday of its builder, Isambard Kingdom Brunel.

328. It was the world's first under-river or subaqueous tunnel. It was supposed to connect the two sides of the London docks, but when it was completed, there was no money left to build the ramps that would take horses and carriages into it, so the tunnel was opened as a tourist attraction (and red-light venue), accessed by stairs. The tunnel was acquired for railway use in the 1860s; today it carries the London Overground *under* the Thames.

329. 'The Signalman' by Charles Dickens.

330. This is the supposed 23 Leinster Gardens, Bayswater. Its neighbour to the right is the supposed 24. They are fake houses, mere facades, designed to preserve the continuity of the elegant stucco terraces in that street. They conceal a cutting of the Metropolitan Railway, created in the mid-1860s as it progressed through West London between Paddington and Kensington. This cutting was ugly in itself; moreover, the steam-condensing locomotives of the Met would take advantage of being briefly in the open air to release steam and smoke. The tunnel of the Met continues below the houses.

331. Because of fears over national security. The government had been warned by Lieutenant General Sir Garnet Wolseley that 'No matter what fortifications and defences were built, there would always be the peril of some continental army seizing the tunnel exit by surprise.' Sir Edward Watkin, chairman of the South Eastern Railway, responded that the cables on the train lifts in the shafts could be cut, trapping any invaders in the tunnel, where they could be drowned at Britain's leisure by deliberately flooding it. But Wolseley won the day.

332. The Severn Tunnel.

333. The tunnel of the Northern Line on the London Underground. It is 17.27 miles long from Morden to East Finchley via Bank. It will be superseded in length by the Woodsmith Mine Tunnel, under construction at the time of writing, that will transport potash from a mine near Whitby to Teesside for processing. This will be 23 miles long, but it won't be a railway tunnel; the potash will be carried on a conveyor belt. The Elizabeth Line is not a contender, since it features only 13 miles of continuous tunnel, and while the Channel Tunnel is 34 miles long, it is not wholly within the UK.

334. A Tube tunnel.

335. The Waterloo & City ('the Drain') and the Victoria. The depot of the latter is above ground.

336. Forty-five per cent.

337. The Severn Tunnel.

338. Two. One is in Wales near Sugar Loaf Station in Powys. The other – now disused – is in the Yorkshire Wolds near Hull.

339. Copenhagen Tunnel, the second one after Gasworks Tunnel north of King's Cross. The tunnel mouth is clearly shown, and it is supposedly below and behind Mrs Wilberforce's house. But the film is disorientating. In one anomalous moment when Mrs Wilberforce answers her front door to Professor Marcus (Alec Guinness), we see the façade of the Midland Grand Hotel over the Professor's shoulder, which suggests she and her house have gravitated towards Bloomsbury. 'Copenhagen Tunnel' is the right answer, however.

340. Clayton Tunnel, on the Brighton main line. The bungalow is thought to have accommodated the functionary in charge of the gas lighting.

341. Ten: eight British, two French.

342. Preserved railways. The Sharpthorne Tunnel is on the Bluebell Railway.

343. One: the Aylsham by-pass tunnel on the 15-inch-gauge Bure Valley Railway in Norfolk. There is also the Cromer Tunnel, built by the Norfolk & Suffolk Joint Railway, but that's now disused.

344. c. Thirty-seven.

345. To test the smoke alarms.

BRIDGES

346. b. It's 3 miles north of the bridge.

347. Twenty-three.

348. The Charing Cross Theatre, previously the Players' Theatre, famous for music hall revival. When the trains went overhead (in the days when it was the Players'), the chairman, and the audience regulars, shouted out, 'To hell with the London, Chatham & Dover Railway!', one of the constituent companies of the South Eastern & Chatham Railway which ran into Charing Cross from 1899 to 1923.

349. Because it blocked views, from the west, of St Paul's. In 1990 the bridge, dating from 1865, was replaced by a tunnel, through which Thameslink trains now run. 'Of all the eyesores of modern London', wrote Walter Thornbury in *Old and New London, Volume One* (1878), 'surely the most hideous is the Ludgate Hill Viaduct – that enormous flat iron that lies across the chest of Ludgate Hill like a bar of metal on the breast of a wretch in a torture chamber.'

350. Hungerford Bridge.

351. Five. The Queen Elizabeth II Bridge (used by the Tyne
& Wear Metro), the High Level (for trains with roadway
beneath, built by Robert Stephenson), the Swing Bridge and
the Tyne Bridge (both for cars) and the Millennium Bridge (for
cyclists and pedestrians).

352. Welwyn Garden City. Queen Victoria opened the viaduct in
1850 but refused an invitation to travel across it in a train.

353. No, but it was a close-run thing. Seventy-three men are
thought to have died during the construction of the Forth
Bridge; seventy-five people are thought to have died when the
Tay Bridge collapsed.

354. Three, after which 'they go back and start all over again'.
According to Dow, twenty men are employed solely on the
painting, but these days the paint jobs last longer – more like
twenty years.

355. Knaresborough. It traverses the river Nidd.

JUNCTIONS

356. Georgemas Junction, where the Far North Line divides for Thurso and Wick, is the most northerly railway junction in Britain.

357. Waterloo East.

358. *The Prime Minister.*

359. Willesden Junction was the inspiration, and the event that occurs at Tenway – the suicide of the villain, Lopez – inspired Tolstoy's depiction of Anna Karenina's suicide.

360. Edward Lear. He wrote a remarkably similar one called 'There Was an Old Man at a Station'.

361. The photograph shows Rugby signal gantry, erected in 1895, dismantled in 1939.

362. Effingham Junction is in Surrey, where the Waterloo–Leatherhead line meets the Waterloo–Guildford; it is not, however (and it is not necessary to know this for a correct answer), in Effingham, but in East Horsley – which is, admittedly, near Effingham.

363. Seventeen.

364. Shaftholme Junction was where the Great Northern Railway's share of the East Coast Main Line gave way to that of the North Eastern Railway.

365. Where lines cross 'at grade', meaning on the same level.

366. The flat crossing is just north of Newark North Gate Station. You will notice the coffee in your cup tremble at that point.

367. Newcastle Station.

368. John Masters.

369. Clapham Junction, the song referring to a girl 'from Clapham'.

ROLLING STOCK

FAMOUS TRAINS

370. *The Irish Mail* (from 1848).

371. *The Cornish Rivera Express*, which for most of its history departed from Platform 1 at Paddington at 10.30 a.m. Things aren't so elemental today. The last time I took this train, it departed from Platform 8 at 10.06.

372. b. 1924.

373. It's true and false, so either answer is correct. In 1897, the *Railway Magazine* familiarly referred to the 10 a.m. Great Western service from Paddington to Cardiff as *The Flying Welshman*, but it never became an official name.

374. From Manchester to Bournemouth, bypassing London. It was named after the pine trees around Bournemouth. The service operated between 1910 and 1967, but was only called *The Pines Express* from 1927.

375. To quote the *Railway Magazine's Encyclopaedia of Titled Trains*, 'This was a real rarity – an officially named train running regularly on the London Underground system.' It departed from South Harrow on the Metropolitan and District railways at 8.15 a.m. and ran to Mansion House.

376. 1928.

377. The crews could access the footplate of the engines by means of a corridor running along the sides of the tenders. This corridor was 5 foot high and 18 inches wide.

378. *The Cheltenham Flyer*.

379. *The Coronation Scot* (London to Scotland on the West Coast Main Line). Not to be confused with *The Coronation* (London to Scotland on the East Coast Main Line), introduced by the LNER in the same year to mark the same event.

380. Called 'Coronation Scot', it was composed by Vivian Ellis in 1938, apparently while on the train between Paddington and Taunton.

381. They are all freight trains.

382. *The Brighton Belle*.

383. *The Bristol Belle*.

384. *The Cathedrals Express*, which was introduced in 1957, and served the cathedral cities of Hereford, Worcester and Oxford – and, come to that, London, since it started from Paddington. The service was stopped in 1965, but the name was recently applied by Great Western to a Class 800 train.

385. The InterCity 125, or High Speed Train, a fast diesel introduced by BR in 1975. Some survive on the network, but they are fading away, to be replaced by bi-mode trains that can switch between electric and diesel power. When the last 125s left Paddington for Exeter on Saturday, 18 May 2019, the train's designer, Sir Kenneth Grange, said, 'All sorts of people have got to know this thing as part and parcel of their life … It's more familiar than their motor car.'

386. Strictly speaking, the answer is the Azuma. That's what Virgin called the bi-mode Class 800s prior to their introduction on the East Coast Main Line, by which time Virgin were no longer involved in the franchise. The trains were launched on the ECML in May 2019 under the auspices of LNER, whose managing director, David Horne, was careful to avoid any unclichéd remarks on the occasion of the launch: 'Setting new benchmarks in rail travel is part of our DNA, and the new Azuma trains are the next big step for LNER in making the customer experience the best it can be.' But 'Class 800' (the official name) is also an acceptable answer. Azuma is Japanese for 'east', which is perhaps why the name was resisted by the Great *Western* Railway, which has also used the Class 800 trains since April 2019.

387. Eurostar. It can reach a speed of 186 mph within the UK.

LOCOMOTIVES

388. 8.4 tons.

389. It was powered by a horse. (The horse walked on a treadmill.)

390. *Sans Pareil*, by Timothy Hackworth.
Perseverance, by Timothy Burstall.
Novelty, by John Ericcson and John Braithwaite.
Rocket, by George and Robert Stephenson.

391. 135.7 tons.

392. Coke.

393. It is 'a single', having only a single pair of driving wheels.
But singles had *big* driving wheels, to maximise adhesion and
speed. This single was by Patrick Stirling, and he created it for
the Great Northern Railway. Stirling singles hauled some of
the fastest trains in Britain in the 1870s. They were displaced
by more powerful engines of the Atlantic type. In *All About
Our British Railways* (1922), G. G. Jackson wrote, 'I do not
know a railwayist who does not share the universal regret that
the single-driver has reached its last phase.'

394. It was Britain's first oil-fired locomotive.

395. On the 15-inch-gauge Romney, Hythe and Dymchurch
Railway in Kent.

396. The King Arthur Class, operated by the LSWR and Southern Railway. The name of one of the engines, *Sir Prianius*, was wrongly spelt. The knight of the same name in *Le Morte d'Arthur* by Sir Thomas Malory was Sir Priamus.

397. b. Saddle tank.

398. A Pacific locomotive is bigger than an Atlantic, just as the Pacific Ocean is bigger than the Atlantic. An Atlantic has a 4-4-2 wheel formation; a Pacific has 4-6-2.

399. Doncaster.

400. A locomotive running without any carriages or wagons.

401. A Black Five.

402. 'Blowing off' – to relieve excess steam pressure.

403. They go tender first (or bunker first in the case of tank engines).

404. Four hundred and eighty-four. All but eight were repaired.

405. The top picture shows a BR Standard Class 9F. These were known as Spaceships by virtue of their size, and their rather airy, disconnected appearance: daylight could be seen between the frame and the boiler. The second picture shows a West Country class locomotive of the Southern Railway, and these were nicknamed Spam Cans on account of their air-smoothed casing, as were the Southern's Battle of Britain class.

406. Smoke deflectors on the smoke box of an engine.

407. The locomotive's boiler exploded, causing the plane to crash, and flinging the pilot into a dyke, where he drowned. No crew or passengers on the train were injured.

408. Henry.

409. 'The Cycling Lion'. It was also known as 'the Starving Lion' because it was thin – and the whole ensemble was also known as 'the ferret and dartboard'. The beautyoftransport.com website observes, 'The good news was that, despite the fact it was neither particularly modern nor in keeping with British Railways corporate typeface … it looked super on British Railways' trains.'

410. *Evening Star.* (It was outsourced from Swindon on the Western Region, and the second ever locomotive to run on the Great Western Railway was called *Morning Star.*)

411. *Tornado*, which was built as an LNER Peppercorn Class A1, and completed in 2008.

412. c. 13,271 (compared to 2,550 diesel locomotives and 3,883 diesel multiple units and railcars).

413. Its name was spelt wrongly. The correction to *Western Legionnaire* was made in 1969.

414. The Deltics or Class 55s, built in 1961 and 1962 for express services on the East Coast Main Line.

415. b. 195.

UNITS

416. The banana. The picture shows one of the aerodynamic railcars introduced onto country branch lines by the GWR from 1932 and known as Flying Bananas. They were wide at the ends, narrow in the middle, and it was this curvature that gave rise to the 'banana' nickname, rather than the colour, which was GWR chocolate and cream, therefore more like a banana sundae than a banana. The 125 HST was also called a 'Flying Banana', but less often.

417. Diesel Multiple Unit. DMUs are well defined by Christian Wolmar in *British Rail: A New History* as 'essentially ... coaches with an engine underneath.'

418. c. Derby Lightweights.

419. Speed whiskers.

420. *The Brighton Belle.*

421. The Isle of Wight, on whose Island Line old Tube trains are used, since they are small enough to fit through a low tunnel at Ryde. The train in the picture dates from 1938.

422. Pacers, which were introduced in 1980. They were built
cheaply and adapted from bus bodies. And they were 'freight-
wagon-inspired'; in other words, they had a wheel at each
corner rather than two four-wheeled bogies, so they were
rough-riding and noisy. As the *Railway Magazine* noted in
September 2019, they were 'not a favourite with regular
commuters'. Pacers were intended as a temporary solution to
rolling stock shortages, but they stuck around. They began to
be phased out in 2019, and have now been entirely withdrawn.
There are concerns that preserved railways might be
overwhelmed with them, since they would be much cheaper
to operate than steam trains.

CARRIAGES

423. A compartment, of which there are none left on ordinary British trains. In *Abroad: British Literary Travelling Between the Wars*, Paul Fussell suggested that an empty compartment was an Englishman's 'idea of heaven'. There may or may not have been a corridor running alongside the compartments.

424. Open seating, which is now universal.

425. The Act stipulated that third-class carriages must be roofed over.

426. Five pounds.

427. In 1892, when the Great Western Railway introduced a train that was gangwayed throughout. Well, it was theoretically possible, were it not for some locked doors. 'The corridors were intended simply to offer lavatory access,' writes Colin Maggs In *Steam Trains*, 'and the gangway connections were locked to prevent third-class passengers sneaking into first-class accommodation.'

428. A clerestory roof. In other words, a raised section of roof, containing windows and ventilators, the main aim being to give more light. Its heyday in Britain was before the First World War. The design was probably last seen in Britain on the 'Q' stock trains of the London Underground District Line (phased out in 1971).

429. A window in a door. The window is opened by lowering it into its housing, hence the name.

430. Moquette. This thick, woollen, carpet-like material is used to cover the seats in most British train interiors, and it is luxurious compared to the plastic, imitation leather or stainless steel frequently used abroad.

431. The west side, so that the window seats were on the *east* side; in other words, to quote from a pamphlet about the train issued by the LNER in 1932, 'on the sea side when it is travelling, as it does for so long continuously, past the magnificent coast scenery between Newcastle and Edinburgh'.

432. It had an observation car at the back that was shaped like a beaver's tail. It was conveyed only in summer, there not being much to see on the East Coast Main Line in winter. It seems to have been crammed with sofas. There were two such cars, and in 1956 they were transferred to the West Highland Line (where there is always something to see). Beaver-tail observation cars originated in America.

433. The dynamometer car placed immediately behind *Mallard* on its record-breaking run of 3 July 1938 for the purpose of recording the speed.

434. Rexine. It was cheap, however: about a quarter of the price of leather, and easier to repair than moquette.

435. A coach comprising more than one class of accommodation. In the British Rail codification of accommodation, 'C' meant composite. The letter 'C' having been thus taken, corridor carriages were designated with the letter 'K'.

436. The LNER. They were highly varnished, however.

437. The first cinema car was introduced in 1935 between King's Cross and Leeds. Sound films were shown by back projection, and the programme lasted an hour. In 1939 the novelty had worn off, and the carriage was converted into a brake van.

438. A coach that could be uncoupled from a train travelling at speed. It would then roll to a halt in a siding under the control of a brakesman. The slip coach had to be at the end of the train, obviously. BR stopped slipping coaches in 1960.

439. False. The highly inventive Oliver Bulleid of the Southern Railway built two double-decked electric units. 'Bulleid's double-deckers lasted for over twenty years,' writes Simon Bradley in *The Railways: Nation, Network and People*, 'grinding around the unglamorous Kentish suburbs on the Dartford loop'.

440. a. British Rail did operate a disco coach, converted in 1973 from a Standard Open carriage, and withdrawn in 1976.

441. *Top of the Pops*.

442. An air-conditioned carriage – i.e. one without openable windows.

443. The 1980s.

444. True, if we use 'Tube' in the strict sense of meaning deep-level lines on the London Underground. The trains on the shallow or 'cut-and-cover' lines now do have air conditioning. Tube trains don't have it because there isn't room for the equipment.

445. c. In 2010. In *The Railways: Nation, Network and People*, Simon Bradley writes that 'the last haunt of the compartment became the 4½-mile long Lymington branch in Hampshire … on which a few 1960s electric units were retained until May 2010.'

446. Metropolitan and Bakerloo.

447. b. 1873, on the North British Railway.

448. It was built for a line of 15-inch gauge – although 'It was very small' will do as an answer. Heywood (an old Etonian) also built a dining car to the same gauge. He was one of the very few aristocrats of his time to have a degree in Applied Science.

449. *Wagons-Lits et des Grands Express Européens*. But *Wagons-Lits* will do.

450. c. In 1928, on the LMS. The accommodation was basic, with no sink in the compartment. On the continent, the berths would have been called couchettes.

451. Snorers and Non-snorers. From *Punch's Library of Railway Humour* (1920).

452. A horizontal bar for hanging trousers was placed above rather than below the curved part for the shoulders of a jacket. This was because men generally remove – and hang up – their jackets before their trousers.

453. Luxury boat trains connecting Plymouth docks with Paddington (and usually not running the other way). They were operated by the Great Western and BR.

454. Graham Greene. The book was *Stamboul Train*, set aboard the variant of the Orient Express that started in Ostend. While writing the book, Greene was dependent for income on selling review copies of novels to Foyles, but *Stamboul Train* became a Book Society choice and was filmed as *Orient Express* in 1933. Greene researched the book by travelling on the train, but he couldn't afford to go all the way to Constantinople, so he got off at Cologne. His characters do go all the way to Constantinople, however.

455. Benjamin Britten wrote the music for *Night Mail*, and a train called *The Benjamin Britten* was named after him. It connected London and Amsterdam (via Harwich and Hook of Holland) by train and ferry, operating by day and night in 1987 and 1988.

456. Victoria, in the days of the boat trains, especially *The Golden Arrow*. The Continental services left from the side of the station built by the London, Chatham & Dover Railway, as opposed to the side built by the London, Brighton and South Coast Railway. In his book *London's Historic Railway Stations* (1972), John Betjeman wrote of the former, 'As though faintly aware that this side of Victoria station is a rather good bit of architecture, the Southern Railway had erected a vast sign in inappropriate lettering – "Gateway to the Continent."'

457. The *Flèche d'Or*, which is 'Golden Arrow' in French.

458. *Steptoe and Son*.

459. Winston Churchill, whose country seat, Chartwell Manor, was nearby.

460. Potties.

46l. Because Ireland has a different track gauge: 5 foot 3 inches.

462. Seaspeed.

463. King's Cross to Edinburgh.

464. Euston to Glasgow.

465. Martin Amis, in his novel, *Night Train*. The passage continues, 'You won't get there so quick, not by natural means. You buy your ticket and you climb on board. That ticket costs everything you have. But it's just one way. This train takes you into the night, and leaves you there. It's the night train.'

466. Eurostar.

467. None. The station was named when it was intended that it would serve the Nightstars – overnight Eurostars that were going to run from the north of England to France and Belgium. They would call at Stratford International on route to the Channel Tunnel, but the Nightstar project was killed off by the rise (apparently unforeseen by the Eurostar people) of budget flights. In 2000 the 139 sleeper cars that had been built for the service were sold to Canada.

FREIGHT

468. Goods trains. Freight was a maritime term, which came from America.

469. Nine Elms, which gave way to Waterloo as the London terminus of the London & South Western Railway. It did have one regular passenger after 1848: Queen Victoria, who found it convenient for Buckingham Palace.

470. Count Dracula, in the novel by Bram Stoker.

471. A charge made by a railway to a customer for failure to unload or discharge a goods wagon on time.

472. A General Utility Van.

473. A Scammell Mechanical Horse, but 'Mechanical Horse' will do. Fifteen thousand were in railway service between the 1930s and the 1960s. Until 2008, the Museum of Rail Travel, operated by the Vintage Carriage Trust at Ingrow, on the Keighley & Worth Valley Railway, exhibited a Mechanical Horse on loan from Tate & Lyle. In 2002, the museum received a speeding ticket from the Greater Manchester Police. It appeared that the Mechanical Horse had been doing 44 mph in a 30 mph zone in Bolton, even though it had a maximum speed of 18 mph and was in pieces in a workshop on the day in question. It transpired that a Belgian car with the same number plate was the true culprit.

474. A train calling at every goods yard along a line (usually a branch line) to collect or deposit goods wagons.

475. A van heated by steam pipes to ripen bananas in transit.

476. c. 96 per cent.

477. Freight revenue was '30–50 per cent higher'.

478. b. By the early 1990s freight revenue was, according to the same source, 'only one quarter of passenger revenue'.

479. Travelling Post Office; the one in question travelled from London to Glasgow.

480. Red Star Parcels, which existed between 1973 and 1991.

BEING A PASSENGER

PASSENGERS IN GENERAL

481. The three prohibited subjects are politics, theology and 'any accident that may chance to have occurred recently'.

482. Anthony Trollope, who wrote while balancing a little tablet or writing slope on his knees.

483. Benjamin Disraeli, in his novel of 1870, *Lothair*. Theodora is speaking.

484. Cicely says it, in *The Importance of Being Ernest* by Oscar Wilde. She is referring to her diary.

485. By timing the speed of the train, which he does by observation of the telegraph posts, which are 60 yards apart, 'and the calculation is a simple one.' (The speed, he announces, is 'fifty-three and a half miles an hour'.)

486. At around that time, smoking compartments were designated 'Smoking', and 'No Smoking' signs were not used except on the South Eastern & Chatham Railway. From 1930, however, the 'No Smoking' designation became widespread and was used in parallel with 'Smoking'. This arose from a ruling by the superintendents of the Railway Clearing House in response to the large number of complaints about passengers smoking in non-smokers.

487. Smoking. A Southern Railway operating instruction dated 8 March 1924 gave the ratio as two-thirds Smoking to one-third Non-smoking. This gradually came down. By 1971, the ratio was fifty-fifty on Inter-City trains, while Non-smoking seats predominated (at 60 per cent) on suburban services.

488. Ladies Only compartments were never mandatory.

489. In 1977, BR was advised that Ladies Only compartments were incompatible with the Sex Discrimination Act of that year.

490. Yes. For example, on Saturday, 5 December 1931, the *Belfast Telegraph* reported that 'The Metropolitan Railway, wishing to move with the times, have reserved two first-class and two third-class compartments, two of them non-smoking and two smoking, exclusively for women in five night trains from Baker Street.'

491. They had a lot of big windows, to make them safe for women.

492. Initially hot water; later on, sodium acetate. In *150 Years of Railway Carriages*, Geoffrey Kitchenside writes that, if the latter were shaken after they had cooled down 'a little more heat seemed to be given out'. Steam heating of carriages eventually took over.

493. a. Sixteen, and eighty-six were under repair.

494. The *Guide* avers that the right 'is vested by custom in the passenger seated next to it, facing the engine'.

495. The Great Western. The company was also famous for signs reading 'Tickets will be Shewn'.

496. The Second World War. The posters were headlined 'CENSORED!' The lyric continued:

> The censor says you must not know
> When there's been a fall of snow.
> That's because it would be <u>news</u>
> The Germans could not fail to <u>use.</u>

497. John Betjeman, in *Summoned by Bells* (1960). The 'we' refers to his boyhood friend, Roland Hughes Wright, with whom Betjeman visited every station on the London Underground, and who subsequently became a monk.

498. *The Rebel.*

499. Paul Theroux, in Chapter One of *The Great Railway Bazaar.*

500. A commuter. The passage is from *Notes from Overground* (1984), by Tiresias (Roger Green).

501. b. There were no ashtrays.

502. In 2007, following the passing of the Health Act of 2006. A ban had been coming in piecemeal since 1980, when smoking was prohibited on the Tyne & Wear Metro.

TIMETABLES AND TIMES

503. 'Bradshaws', as the timetables were known, were the brainchild of George Bradshaw. They appeared in monthly instalments, and Bradshaw, a strict Quaker, didn't want to give publicity to heathen deities so, in his early timetables, January (for example) was referred to as 'First Month'. *Bradshaws* were notoriously hard to understand. *Punch* magazine's 'Tourist's Alphabet', as collected in *Punch's Library of Humour* (1920), begins,

> A is the affable guard whom you square
> B is the *Bradshaw* which leads you to swear.

504. A timetable with destinations listed in alphabetical order. It was London-centric but more user-friendly than a Bradshaw. 'I would sooner lose a train by the *ABC* than catch it by *Bradshaw*,' said Oscar Wilde. It is not to be confused with the *ABC* booklets of locomotive numbers published for trainspotters by Ian Allan.

505. True, and it was the standard time in Britain by the 1850s.

506. Henry James (quoted in *The Legend of the Master* by Simon Nowell-Smith).

507. Oscar Wilde. He was being transferred from Wandsworth Gaol to Reading Gaol, handcuffed and in prison uniform. 'A crowd formed' writes Richard Ellmann in his biography of Wilde, 'first laughing and then jeering at him. One man recognised that this was Oscar Wilde and spat at him.'

508. *Hilda Lessways*, by Arnold Bennett.

509. It happened at 11 a.m. on Tuesday, 11 November to mark the first anniversary of the Armistice. According to the *Railway Magazine*, 'many a touching sight was witnessed in railway trains and at stations, the remembrance of which will not soon pass from the memories of those who witnessed or participated in them.'

510. Paddington. It's three-faceted; the other three are four-faceted.

511. A service whose trains departed at the same minutes to or from the hour; or, ideally, *on* the hour.

512. The missing word is 'watch'. 'Rarely did a fireman challenge the driver's version of the time,' added McKenna, 'for to do so was to call into question the traditional relationship between the two men.' A relative of a man who'd driven steam locomotives on the East Coast Main Line told the author of this book that the man never wore a watch after the day of his retirement.

513. Will Hay, as William Porter, the out-of-his-depth station master of Buggleskelly in the film *Oh, Mr Porter!* The title comes from a music-hall song.

514. Miss the one before.

515. Timetables that include freight as well as passenger trains.

516. *4.50 From Paddington.*

517. 1964, although Frank Pick, second in command at London Transport, had wanted London Underground to make the switch as early as 1931. As he wrote in a letter to *The Times* that year, 'The transit of the sun across the meridian has no visible significance underground.'

518. Aberdeen to Penzance (or vice versa), the service provided by the company named CrossCountry (with no gap between the words). The journey is over 1,000 miles and takes 25 hours.

519. 'Timetables for what?'

CLASSES

520. The Duke of Wellington, who hated trains.

521. 'Stanhope' was a corruption of 'stand up'.

522. The Regulation of Railways Act, 1844, required companies to run at least one train a day for third-class passengers. Any slow local train came to be called the 'Parly' by railway staff, the Act having been passed by Parliament.

523. The Midland Railway, in 1872. In the process of this rationalisation, it made its Third Class more luxurious. Other companies gradually followed suit, and by 1930 Second Class was mainly gone.

524. c. 96 per cent.

525. It was, according to J. Allan Rannie, writing in the *Railway Magazine* of May 1935, 'the solitary occasion when Watson travelled Third'. He was accompanying the miserly Josiah Amberley, who had insisted on Third Class.

526. 1941. In the war, we were all supposed to be 'in it together'. There never had been classes on the deep-level, or Tube, lines. Well, not unless one counts the anomalous case of the Great Northern & City Railway, which opened in 1904 (Finsbury Park to Moorgate), and which might be classed as a Tube but which had bigger tunnels than the other Tubes, hence the nickname 'Big Tube'. It had luxurious trains which, between 1916 and 1934, had class divisions. The Central London Railway (which became the Central Line) planned to have classes but abandoned the idea just before opening in 1900, although the company had built its carriages by then, so some seats were in effect First Class.

527. 1987.

528. No. The principle was established in Jones v. Great Northern Railway (1918), in which a first-class passenger was denied compensation for 'second-class irruption'.

TICKETS

529. An Edmondson ticket. These were cardboard tickets of about $^{13}/_{16}$ by $2\frac{1}{4}$ inches and named after their inventor, a sometime station master on the Newcastle & Carlisle Railway, Thomas Edmondson (1792–1852). The tickets were consecutively numbered and had the start and end points pre-printed, to prevent fraud by ticket clerks.

530. 1989.

531. To create a child's ticket (half fare) A vertical snip created a single, a diagonal a return. This method was also used for other half fares, e.g. for bicycles and dogs.

532. Ticket clippers or nippers; Edmondson sold them in conjunction with his tickets. 'The Ticket Nipper is chiefly used to show that the railway ticket has passed examination at a certain station,' states an early Edmondson catalogue, 'or to cancel the ticket altogether'.

533. Because the passengers' names used to be entered in a book; and in the early days, travellers 'booked' a ticket. In *The Railways: Nation, Network and People*, Simon Bradley observes that to 'buy' a ticket seems to be a post-Victorian usage.

534. The Central London Railway, which opened in 1900 (Shepherd's Bush to Bank), on which all fares originally cost 2d.

A cartoon in *Punch* depicted the following exchange at a booking office counter:

> Intemperate passenger: 'Hi, guv'nor, there ain't no station named on this ticket!'
> Ticket clerk: 'No; all our tickets are alike.'
> Intemperate passenger: 'Then, 'ow do I know where I'm going?'

535. A ticket issued at a discounted fare, or free, to a railway employee and (sometimes) his or her family.

536. The Flying Squad.

537. A pensioner entitled to concessionary fares after 9.30 a.m. They tended to turn up at the ticket office at 9.15 asking, 'Am I too early?' A crueller designation for them was 'vultures'.

538. b. 2003.

REFRESHMENTS

539. 1879. It was a Pullman carriage on a Great Northern train between Leeds and King's Cross.

540. 'Don't know I'm sure, sir. I've only been here a fortnight.'

541. '*Would* you mind taking them into the *second-class* refreshment room?'

542. Anthony Trollope.

543. Swindon, which opened in 1842 on the Great Western Main Line. The contractors who built the station provided what is considered the first railway refreshment room. They did not charge the GWR directly for this but allowed the company to lease the premises for 1d per year, subject to a clause whereby all trains passing Swindon must stop for ten minutes so that passengers might take refreshment. Of course, it was not obligatory to take refreshment, but it would be expensive for anyone who did so. From 1895 this agreement began to be breached in the case of express trains.

544. Isambard Kingdom Brunel.

545. Charles Dickens. The story is called 'The Boy at Mugby', and for 'Mugby' read Rugby. Dickens had been turfed off a train there one evening (the train having caught fire). He and his agent went into the refreshment room for a coffee, and Dickens began drinking his before the agent had handed over the money. For this, Dickens was loudly reprimanded by the manageress of the refreshment room, and her assistant, a boy, laughed. So Dickens – a rather touchy man – made the boy an unsympathetic character in his story.

546. It was the 'Flying Scotsman Cocktail', created by Harry Craddock, steward of the Savoy Hotel's American bar to celebrate the launch of the non-stop *Flying Scotsman* service in 1928. It was also available on the train, along with other cocktails, including Silver Streak, Hoola-Hoola, Monkey Glan and Leave-It-To-Me.

547. *Brideshead Revisited*. Charles Ryder is going to Brideshead for the second time. Compare William Boot's journey in the opposite direction (towards Paddington) in Waugh's much better novel, *Scoop*:

> He went to the dining car and ordered some whisky. The steward said 'We're serving teas. Whisky after Reading.' After Reading he tried again. 'We're serving dinners. I'll bring you one to your carriage.' When it came, William spilled it down his tie.

548. Half a million.

549. The Betjeman Arms at St Pancras International Station.

550. One bottle of wine or four cans of beer. Spirits are not allowed. The author of the present book has often breached those limits with impunity.

551. c. 250.

552. Victoria Wood.

553. Great Western. 'Naturally, they are a bit of a secret,' wrote Michael Williams in *The Trains Now Departed* – 'scarcely advertised and with an atmosphere that has something of the mystique of a London gentleman's club'.

EROTICA

554. The young Isambard Kingdom Brunel. The accident was the flooding of the Thames Tunnel, which was being built by his father, Marc.

555. George Stephenson, after he had given her a ride on the footplate of his engine *Rocket,* just prior to the opening of the Liverpool–Manchester Railway.

556. *The Pickwick Papers* by Charles Dickens.

557. Marie Lloyd. The song includes the line, 'She'd never had her ticket punched before.' Her other song with a railway theme, and slightly subtler innuendo, was 'Oh, Mr Porter!'

558. Compartment stock.

559. c. Twenty-four. And her mother ran a brothel in Cincinnati.

560. Cannon Street and Charing Cross, so the shuttle was a popular way of getting from the City to the West End.

561. A: *It Always Rains on Sunday* (1947), described on the website Movie-Locations.Com as 'a darker twin to *Brief Encounter*'. Temple Mills had started life as a wagon works of the Great Eastern Railway. Under BR, it became a marshalling yard. Today, part of the site is occupied by the Eurostar Engineering Centre.

562. A (or the) train enters a tunnel.

563. *Love on a Branch Line*.

564. Shirley Williams.

ACCIDENTS

565. c. About one in 420,000.

566. William Huskisson, MP, at the opening of the Liverpool–Manchester Railway. He was run over by Robert Stephenson's engine, *Rocket*. Huskisson is often said to be the first victim of a steam-powered railway accident, but in February 1813 a thirteen-year-old boy, John Bruce, was killed on the Middleton Railway, a coal-carrying line in Leeds, while running enthusiastically alongside its locomotive, *Salamanca*. There is a statue of Huskisson in a lonely little park, Pimlico Gardens, by the Thames in SW1.

567. *The Wrong Box*, and the levity is maintained even though people die in the accident.

568. *Our Mutual Friend*. The postscript to the novel reads,

> On Friday the 9th of June in the present year, Mr and Mrs Boffin (in their manuscript dress of receiving Mr and Mrs Lammle at breakfast) were on the South Eastern Railway with me, in a terribly destructive accident. When I had done what I could do to help others, I climbed back into my carriage – nearly turned over a viaduct, and caught almost on the turn – to extricate the worthy couple. They were much soiled, but otherwise unhurt.

569. Charles Dickens died. It is said he never fully recovered from the Staplehurst accident. He did travel on trains afterwards but would grip the armrest of his seat tightly, fearing that the carriage was 'down on the right-hand side'.

570. Jilly Cooper, who was in the Paddington train crash, in which thirty-one people died. Ten years after the event, she told the *Stroud Examiner*, 'I went to the Savoy to clean up a bit, and a kind lady gave me a pashmina to hide the blood.'

571. The collapse of the Tay Bridge. The engine fell into the Tay when the bridge collapsed amid a storm at 7 p.m. on 28 December 1879. All seventy-five people on the train died. No. 224 was recovered after three months on the bed of the Firth of Tay, and it was known to the footplate crews who drove it in subsequent years as 'the Diver'. It would be satisfying to write that the engine found its way to a preserved railway, where its duties include hauling Santa Specials and other jolly outings, but it was scrapped in 1919. The number plate from the tender is preserved at Halliwell's House Museum, Selkirk.

572. Two hundred and twenty-seven people died at Quintinshill.

573. Five.

574. *Accident*. 'If we really wanted to find a British railway novel capable of being installed in some literary pantheon,' writes Ian Carter in *Railways and Culture in Britain*, 'then Arnold Bennett's *Accident* provides the best candidate.'

575. Signal Passed at Danger.

576. The Southern Railway, the speaker being Sir Herbert Walker.

577. In 1951, when two trains of the Far Tottering & Oyster Creek Branch Railway, designed by Rowland Emett and running along the South Bank in London as part of the Festival of Britain, collided. The FT&OCR was based on a series of railway cartoons Emett had drawn for *Punch*.

578. Walking along a track with one's back to oncoming traffic.

COLOUR SECTION

579. Green.

580. Black, white and canary yellow, which brings to mind a joke.

> Q: What goes a hundred miles an hour on railway lines
> and is yellow and white?
> A: A railwayman's egg sandwich.

581. The Somerset & Dorset Joint Railway.

582. So they could be waved as danger signals in an emergency.

583. Southern Railway = Malachite Green.
Great Western = Brunswick Green.
North British Railway = Bronze Green.
London, Brighton & South Coast Railway = Improved Engine
    Green.
London & North Eastern Railway = Apple Green (the shade
    was also known as Grass Green).

584. Because it was so dark it struck many people as black. It has
been compared to the colour of oil spilled on a road.

585. Umber and cream.

586. The Southern, because its engines, carriages and stations were
all green.

587. The Glasgow Underground Railway. Because the trains are circular and orange, as is the line.

588. True.

589. False. 'Plum and spilt milk' is an old LNWR livery, although it was also employed briefly by BR.

590. a. Garter Blue.

591. c. Indian Red.

592. The Midland, and the London, Midland & Scottish.

593. The Great Western.

594. Green.

595. The Blue Pullman.

596. Misha Black. Rail Blue was also known as Monastral Blue.

597. Blue and dirt.

598. 1938: Red.
1959: Grey (or, as London Underground liked to say, silver).
1992: Red, white and blue.

ANSWERS

599. Yellow Trains are, to quote from a *Railway Magazine* advertisement for a book about them, 'the various measurement and test trains operated by Network Rail'.

600. The London Overground, after its colour on the Tube map, which is orange.

PICTURE CREDITS

The author and publisher wish to thank the following for the kind permission to include the photographs in this book, as follows:

Alamy: Q. 19 FLHC15 / Alamy Stock Photo, Q. 80 GL Archive / Alamy Stock Photo, Q. 405 (bottom) Peter Moulton / Alamy Stock Photo, Q. 428 Washington Imaging / Alamy Stock Photo, Q. 577 Chronicle / Alamy Stock Photo; **Antiques Trade Gazette**: Q. 294; **Author photos**: Q. 7, Q. 12, Q. 268, Q. 275, Q. 317, Q. 330, Q. 393, Q. 397, Q. 402, Q. 409, Q. 416, Q. 418, Q. 421, Q. 423, Q. 424, Q. 473, Q. 495, Q. 529; **Bodmin & Wenford Railway** Q. 142; **Flickr**: Q. 39 mikeyashworth, Q. 571 from bellrockman2011, Q. 595 from Nashphoto, Q. 561 from AndyHoare; **Getty**: Q. 241 Fox Photos / Stringer, Q. 395 Fox Photos, Q. 371 Topical Press Agency / Stringer; **Herald and Times/Newsquest Media Group**: Q. 278; **London Transport Museum**: Q. 133; **Public domain**: Q. 119; Q. 367; **Science & Society**: Q. 326; **Warwickshire County Records Office**: Q. 361; **Wikipedia**: Q. 176; Q. 217 from Jonathunder, CCBY-SA 3.0; Q. 266 from G-13114, CCBY-SA 3.0; Q. 340 from cupcakekid CCBY-SA 3.0; Q. 355 from Jo Turner / Mallard on Knaresborough viaduct / CCBY-SA 2.0; Q. 405 (top) from Ben Brooksbank CCBY-SA 2.0

While every effort has been made to contact copyright-holders of illustrations, the author and publishers would be grateful for information about any illustrations where they have been unable to trace them, and would be glad to make amendments in further editions.